THE
GULLIBILITY
GAP

by the same author:
The Bad Food Guide (1967)
The Beverage Report (1970)
Skye (1970)

THE GULLIBILITY GAP

BY DEREK COOPER

illustrated by Michael Edwards

Routledge & Kegan Paul

London and Boston

First published in 1974
by Routledge & Kegan Paul Ltd
Broadway House, 68–74 Carter Lane,
London EC4V 5EL and
9 Park Street,
Boston, Mass. 02108, USA
Set in Monotype Plantin
and printed in Great Britain by
Clarke, Doble & Brendon Ltd
Plymouth

ISBN 0 7100 7972 9
Library of Congress Catalog Card No. 74–81312

CONTENTS

INTRODUCTION

A notable fact about Space Age Man is that the further the frontiers of knowledge are extended the more he is disposed to turn his back on reality. It is not without significance that in the same year Neil Armstrong took his giant leap forward for Mankind, Man in his role of credulous ape took an equally giant step backward—two million *ouija* boards were sold in the USA alone.

Padding along behind the human traveller on his gullible journey through life is a mind-bending experience. If you pay close attention to the correspondence columns of popular papers and magazines you will find revealed a quite extraordinary sub-world of dottiness. Popular delusion is scaling new heights of lunacy.

'Our first parents—Adam and Eve—were white', states a letter in the *Daily Mail*. 'How then did the coloured races come into existence? This intriguing question baffles me.'

A young girl signing herself 'Hopeful' writes to agony columnist Marjorie Proops in *Woman's Mirror*: 'Dear Marje, if a girl has intercourse and then has nothing more to do with boys for a year, can she become a virgin again?' A *News of the World* reader asks if she can 'say a few words that should completely

A*

remove fear of ghosts? The information has been given to me by ghosts. If you are privileged to see a ghost do not bolt like a frightened animal; take an intelligent interest in it, talk to it and ask if you can be of help in any way. There is some reason for the appearance and YOU may be the one appointed to help.'

A man writes to share his formula for winning football pools with other *News of the World* readers: 'When I've filled in my soccer coupon I lay it on a plate and sprinkle a little nutmeg powder on it. Then I leave it for 20 hours before posting it.'

An Irish woman informs the editor of the *Belfast News Letter* that she possesses a pet budgerigar which has a swing in its cage: 'I have made a practice of disconnecting this swing each Sunday and not putting it back into use until Monday morning. Is this in accord with strict Christian principle?'

The members of the Panacea Society of Bedford take space in the national papers to tell Britain what the Bible says about the Box. 'Crime & Banditry, Distress of Nations & Perplexity will continue to increase', they announce, 'until the Bishops open Joanna Southcott's Box of sealed writings.' On another page there is intelligence that General Amin has seen a flying saucer and a warning to those born under the sign of Scorpio not to travel on Friday. In California, acting on the prognostications of a crystal-gazer, thousands have taken to the hills to await the final rupture of the San Andreas Fault. A Thames Ditton reader claims that the plan to put fluoride in his water supply is masterminded by the henchmen of the Kremlin, a Soviet conspiracy to sap the occipital areas of the Anglo-Saxon brain. In São Paulo a Roman Catholic priest gives weekly open-air demonstrations of levitation, and in Leningrad a housewife is able to make objects move without touching them.

The eccentric events chronicled in the pages that follow are a tribute not only to Man's epic credulity but also to his innate and monumental optimism.

ONE

THE LAND OF MAKE BELIEVE

I suppose most of us can recall the few seminal flashes of insight in our lives without effort. My first lesson in the school of hard knocks occurred at 6.16 a.m. on the morning of 25 December 1932. Out of my pillowslip tumbled the Big Present. I sat holding it stunned with excitement. On the cover of the box an artist had drawn the contents—a golden Pullman express flashed down the permanent way, steam streaming from its stack; it was passing a GWR tank locomotive hauling coal wagons, a breakdown crane, timber camions, cattle trucks and a van from out of which leant a kindly flag-waving guard. Further down the line a passenger train in LMS livery waited at a busy country station—there must have been forty yards of track embellished with viaducts, bridges, level crossings, turn-tables and signal boxes. How, I wondered, could they get all that in such a small box and how was I going to get everyone out of the dining room after breakfast to set it all up?

When I pulled off the lid the answer was painfully revealed. One small clockwork engine, two carriages, ten pieces of straight track and six curved—I could have laid the whole lot out in the cupboard under the stairs without removing the carpet sweeper. For the rest of Christmas Day I paid particular attention to boxes

and tins. I noted with a deepening sense of betrayal that on the lid the Moroccan dates looked plump and gleaming—inside they were shrunken and stringy; the raspberries we had for tea were just a pulpy mass, not the splendid bursting berries some illusionist had drawn on the can.

Things have not changed in the last forty years; in fact television has enhanced the opportunities for distortion. When it comes to concocting commercials for the food industry all manner of strange devices are used. Mashed potato is sometimes substituted for ice cream because ice cream melts too quickly under the studio floodlights. Steam rising from a pie just as mother baked it is all too often cigarette smoke. Glycerine is brushed on cheese to make it gleam; coloured water or whisky is used in tea commercials because tea has an oily film on its surface.

But surely we know all these things; we know that the picture of the Family Beef Steak Pie on the packet is a glamorised fraud—nothing like the bland and stodgy product inside? Surely we all know that they put Eno's in the wine to make it sparkle on our screens larger than life? Isn't it common knowledge that they squeeze detergent in the soup to give it those delicious bubbles?

Not very different from the way in which many house agents squeeze the most out of what they have to sell. So cocooned in fantasy is the average description of a property that you need a key to crack the code. We were once sent by one of these masters of hyperbole to view a cottage in the Cotswolds. We should have guessed what it was going to be like when he said, 'You won't need a key, the door is . . . open.'

When we got there we found he was quite right. Not only was the door open, it was down and out, lying like a duckboard on the rotting floor. The roof was open too; we could see the sky through the ancient sagging thatch.

'This can't be the place,' my wife said, 'I mean this isn't a house, it's a ruin.' I pulled the estate agent's blurb out of my pocket: 'Charmingly romantic period farmhouse in highly sought-after Cotswold hamlet. Ideal for conversion £14,500.' We looked around the crumbling rooms. There was a 'wealth of beams' all right, most of them collapsed on what was left of the upper floors. Grass sprouted through the 'mullioned library' floor. One good shove with a bulldozer would have converted it into a mound of rubble—ideal for infilling the new by-pass which we found (just by chance) was going to run through the 'olde worlde paddock'.

How could anybody in their right mind have described that wreck as an 'immensely appealing residence of character'? But nobody is more of an optimist than the dedicated house agent. If you're standing next to him in a pub you may be holding a half-*empty* glass of beer—he'll be holding a half-*full* one.

In the months that followed, other agents sent us to see houses which were invariably lavishly appointed, spacious, gracious, superb, outstanding, unique, unrivalled, delightful, immaculate, ideal, wonderful, substantial, superior and, invariably, appalling. We soon found that there was a whole repertoire of totally meaningless words which were just sprinkled through the advertisements like so much verbal dolly mixture; something to soften you up for the grim realities you were about to inspect.

We just didn't seem to be talking the same language. One morning I received details of an 'imposing Edwardian residence situate upon rising ground'. I rang the agent.

'This house, the one with no garage,' I said.

'*Ah yes sir, the quality residence with ample space for double garage.*'

'The one miles from the station.'

'*You mean the one a short stroll from the Tube?*'

'It's got this nasty backyard.'

'*The bijou town patio sir?*'

'You say it's "situate on rising ground". Does that mean that it's also situate on *falling* ground?'

There was a long silence at the other end of the 'phone. After that we didn't get any more details through the post. I reckon we'd been put down as troublemakers.

But other agents were keen to despatch us to inspect all manner of rubbish. There was the depressing Victorian villa which had 'a pleasant shuttered elevation'; the owner had nailed two mauve shutters to an upper window. As one of the shutters had slipped the house looked pop-eyed, like an old tart with a fallen eyelash.

Just as secondhand car dealers have a patter to move cars which no one would buy unless the balance of their mind was disturbed, so house agents have a special alphabet of exaggeration. Words like:

LOVABLE   As in 'lovable artisan's cottage'. A dwelling the size of a doll's house suitable only for persons of restricted growth.

4

SECLUDED Completely cut off from all light by surrounding highrise flats and blank wall of precision engineering works facing the kitchen window.

FAVOURED Upwind of the soap works and leather tannery.

CENTRAL Downwind of ditto.

CONVENIENT Opposite ditto.

QUICK SALE Owner anxious to complete before you can get a surveyor round to confirm that the entire fabric is riddled with dry rot, rising damp, woodworm and terminal subsidence.

EASY TO RUN Rooms so small that you can't get a vacuum cleaner through the door. See also COMPACT and LABOURSAVING.

MANY ORIGINAL FEATURES See also FULL OF CHARACTER. Nobody has bothered to remove the gas brackets in the hall. Completely neglected and unimproved—see FINE EXAMPLE OF ITS PERIOD.

COMMANDING VIEWS You can see the roofs of thousands and thousands of identical houses from the boxroom window if you stand on a chair.

BACHELOR FLAT Bedsitting room with use of gas ring.

REDECORATED THROUGHOUT BY ARTIST OWNER Black ceilings, dung-coloured loo, purple psychedelic sitting room. Other warning words to watch for are TASTEFUL, UNUSUAL, BOLD and NOVEL.

FASTIDIOUSLY MAINTAINED Has a frilly pink mat on the lavatory seat.

NEEDS SOME ATTENTION Needs rewiring, replumbing, reproofing, repointing, etc. See also WOULD SUIT ACTIVE COUPLE, UNLIMITED POSSIBILITIES FOR ENTHUSIAST, IDEAL INVESTMENT.

QUIET SITTING TENANTS An atrocious old couple good for another twenty-five years who will make your life an absolute hell until you give them £4,000 to leave.

VILLAGE ATMOSPHERE Working-class slum infiltrated by hippies, heads and media couples.

QUIET COUNTRYSIDE   Three buses a week.

UNSPOILT COUNTRYSIDE   Two buses a week.

DEEP COUNTRYSIDE   No buses.

IDYLLIC RURAL RETREAT   Inaccessible except on foot and in wellies. No electricity, mains water or telephone. Cut off for most of the winter. See also OLDE WORLDE HAVEN, ISOLATED DREAM HOME and TIRED OF THE RAT RACE?

LUXURY   As in 'luxury Georgian-style executive maisonette'—not cheap.

ULTRA-MODERN   Ugly.

ROOMY CONSERVATORY   A draughty extension which probably contains an old mangle. Run up by a former occupant to house his motor bike and sidecar. See also SUNPARLOUR, ELEGANT GARDEN ROOM.

UTILITY ROOM   A room too small to get a bed in.

RAMBLING   Designed by a jobbing builder and full of long dark passages leading nowhere. Not to be confused with rambling as in RAMBLING GARDEN. This means overgrown and full of rubbish.

WELL-MATURED   Well-matured fruit trees are trees which are so old they no longer bear fruit. Well-matured elms are elms which are about to fall on the house and flatten it. Well-matured grounds means a nasty garden which has been poisoned by soot and cats and is so stricken that not even a nettle will grow.

SHORT WALK   As in 'short walk from shops and schools'. House agents are notoriously athletic men and a short walk for them could be anything up to five miles. The usual interpretation is a ninepenny bus-ride or the distance one woman could push one pram in one hour.

USEFUL RANGE OF OUTBUILDINGS   A half-filled-in Anderson shelter, a creosoted shed full of old paint brushes and jars of rusty nails, a concrete bunker full of coal dust.

Although we ought to know that when the house agent says that he 'enthusiastically recommends' something he is really saying that he's been trying to get rid of it for months; although we know that buying a different armpit deodorant isn't going to bring passion into our lives and that the furniture will still look shabby however long we rub it with Wonderpol (plus added Sparklex), the greater the distortion, the more gullible we become.

Perhaps we have a deep need to be duped; maybe we really want to inhabit the world the agency men peddle where everyone is always healthy, young and dazzlingly attractive. And although we know that no vacuum cleaner will make our carpets brighter, no meat cube will turn a tasteless stew into a gastronomic banquet, we are content to believe that miracles with 3p off may occur.

When the late Roy Brooks tried to sell houses warts and all, deliberately pointing out their defects in a series of pejorative advertisements, he found, so conditioned were househunters not to believe the truth, that all-night queues began to form at his office door.

His witty deprecation rebounded tenfold. What other agents couldn't unload with gushing praise, Brooks moved with exaggerated damns. The formula was the same: the prospectus sells, not the property.

Brooks sold a lot of stuff by moving potential customers to laughter; a change from the old technique of sale by fear. Fear of being thought socially inadequate (*Are* you *gagged by the old school tie?*) or ill-educated (*Rush me my FREE morocco-bound, gold-tooled library of Great Masters of World Thought*) or not giving your children the right start in life (*Get the Children's Book of Knowledge now—you owe it to them!*) or your loved one the right end (*There's deep consolation . . . serene through shower or heavy rain . . . for those who know the casket of a dear one is protected against water in the ground by a Clark Metal Grave Vault*).

Fear of smelling (*Bidex doesn't just cover up odour: it prevents it*); fear of not smelling (*If deep inside you want to be loved as quiet things are loved, shouldn't your perfume be Je Reviens?*); fear

7

of having blemished feet *(A Scholl girl isn't just a pretty face. Feet are getting nicer)*; fear of being undistinguished *(Lord Calvert is the whiskey preferred by so many of America's most distinguished men)*.

In its quest to make the consumer more acquisitive, advertising tends to feed him all kinds of ideas which he might not have thought of himself. Maybe, left to his own devices, motoring man wouldn't want to be first away at the lights. But a large slice of the carmakers' advertising revenue goes in persuading people that they need to be out front. Doubtless few cars in production are more desirable than the 132 mph three litre BMW sports coupé. What company director or rising young executive could resist the appeal of the full-page advertisement which appeared in the *Financial Times* when the car was launched:

> . . . ride new power, ride new surge, ride new obedience. Indulge in concise control comfort—a merger of man mind machine into one.
>
> Burst the barriers that bend ordinary mortals into one choking mass of mediocrity. Break out into a motoring experience that leaves you where you should be. King.
>
> Ride the new one from the land of the Valkyries . . .

You might have thought from the hysteria of the hand-crafted poesy that they were purveying a Wagnerian magic chariot and not just a £5,464 car with four wheels, a heated rear window and a 6-cylinder in-line unique triple hemisphere swirl-action combustion power unit.

Copywriting has for many years inhabited a never-never land in which we are not supposed to *believe* what we are told, only behave as if we did. This is *Depth Charge*, 'the foam bath that got its secrets from the sea':

> We've stolen the sea. From a South Sea lagoon we took the colour of deepest blue. We stole the fragrance from a gentle sea breeze. And the foam from a breaking wave. From tiny sea-plants we took minerals that tingle, sparkle and rejuvenate. And finally we stole the ocean's mystery. Its power and excitement.

8

Mystery, magic and secrecy still play a powerful part in advertising. The contents of the bottle may look prosaic in the laboratory analysis but you should see them on the printed page. Hark to: *Windsor Gold (the bathway to beauty)*:

Six golden beauty preparations. Each blended with a secret distillation of bitter sweet and potent Alpine herbs and the rare mysterious Ginseng plant from the foothills of the Himalayas . . . now you *know* your body is beautiful. You are ready for the day. Or night. Or Anything.

Rare, mysterious ginseng? It grows fairly freely in China and Korea, and the only thing faintly mysterious about it is that though the Chinese have prized the medicinal properties of its roots for centuries, there is not a single shred of evidence that it has any therapeutic properties whatsoever.

Far more mysterious than ginseng is the way in which the agency wordsmiths can transmute dross into purest fairy gold. Most of the food we eat today is processed in vast automated factories and masterminded not by cooks but by chemists, physicists and quality controllers. This fact of life has not yet filtered through to the advertising men who still believe that tinned and packeted products are actually made by fat smiling chefs who lend a touch of *haute cuisine* by association. Many of these chefs are got up to look like the public's idea of Escoffier or Carême so you will think when scanning the advertising copy for Scrumpiwhip (the golden dessert with golden profits) that a gastronomic genius had his finger on the factory button.

To advertise their packet soup Symingtons use a distinguished-looking citizen in chef's garb who sports authoritative black-rimmed spectacles and an upper lip adorned with a well-trimmed Parisian moustache. He is depicted beside an old-fashioned gas stove with several bubbling saucepans and a chopping board on which are some mushrooms and parsley. It is not quite clear from the advertisement whether he is meant to be preparing the firm's entire output on this small stove or whether he has just reconstituted them from a gallon pack.

In the same way patently dehydrated and processed food can be described as if that moment it had been picked in the orchard or dug from the soil. Key words with healthy rural connotations (*harvest, country, spring, farm-fresh, dew-drenched, dawn-gathered, sun-kissed, summer-ripened*) are employed, often basely, to dignify a product which may be manufactured from almost totally synthetic ingredients.

America, which has been exposed to this kind of verbal chicanery for longer than we have, is at last mounting a rearguard action. Recently the US Federal Trade Commission and America's angriest consumer, Ralph Nader, felt that Colonel Morton's Kentucky-style lemon cream pie should change its name—or its contents. The pie contained no lemon, no cream and no eggs (the traditional ingredients of a lemon cream pie) but was fabricated from such sundry good things as guar gum, sodium caseinate, monosodium phosphate, polysorbate 60, mono- and di-glycerides, lecithin, corn syrup, shortening and starch and registered under US Patent No. 3202114. Dear old Colonel Morton alias the Continental Baking Company, whose artificial frozen dessert was a best-selling line, were understandably dismayed that anyone could put such a literal interpretation on words.

There is virtually no field where the euphoric lunacy of the adman hasn't penetrated. What is perhaps alarming is that being found out seems to have no effect. Holiday-makers return again and again to seaside resorts which in reality are as unlike the travel operator's description as Southend is like St Tropez.

In 1973 nearly 26 million holiday-makers went to Spain from various parts of Europe, most of them on package tours sold through the medium of thick and glossy brochures, brochures which might make even an estate agent blush. One big British operator reckons that it takes eight brochures to sell a holiday and as eight brochures may cost anything up to £2 to print and distribute they have to embody selling skill of a high degree. Entering the sunshine world of the travel brochure is a heady experience. Every village is quaint, every view panoramic, every beach of golden sand. No mistrals or tramontanes blow, no rain falls, the bougainvillea is in perpetual bloom, and your fellow guests are specimens of unique and irresistible physical beauty. Where all the fat old people go for holidays I've never found out.

Perhaps Benidorm is like Bath in the days of Mr Pickwick and Angelo Cyrus Bantam, an early practitioner of the dismal art of public relations. 'Mr Pickwick,' said A. C. Bantam, 'Do you see the lady in the gauze turban?'

'The fat old lady?' inquired Mr Pickwick innocently.

'Hush, my dear sir—nobody's fat or old in Ba-ath.'

In the last decade there has been so much building in Spain that villages change almost overnight—a circumstance which might charitably provide an excuse for the inaccuracy of many brochures, when they begin to rhapsodise about the beauties of individual Spanish resorts.

The ordinary holiday-maker may be gulled, but the reputable travel agent should know exactly what a resort is like. A series of devastatingly honest gazetteers has been compiled (by Continental Hotel Gazetteers, Beaconsfield, Bucks.) giving the real lowdown on holiday resorts, and it's interesting to compare these with the imaginative descriptions of the brochures. One big operator has described Malgrat on the Costa Brava as: 'A bathing paradise of blue sea combined with the golden sand, cloudless skies, interesting shops, bars and gay cafés where one can only be serenely satisfied.'

The gazetteer described Malgrat as 'A small one-horse town with one long street of indifferent shops. The railway line runs parallel with the entire length of the beach without the benefit of a protecting fence. The beach itself is of the usual small stones— altogether not the best resort for very young children.'

Benidorm fares no better. One of the most widely visited resorts on the Costa Blanca, it is, according to a brochure: '. . . truly modern with fine tall hotels pushing upwards into a deep blue sky. The quaint, flower-decked fishermen's cottages cluster round the blue-domed church and the streets are filled with tiny shops and cosy bars.' And how attractive it sounds! But the gazetteer regarded Benidorm with a less enthusiastic eye: 'Nearly submerged in the centre of a vortex of concrete, dust and juke boxes lies the little old village and port of Benidorm. Here one may purchase souvenirs by the million and in the numerous cafés such local delicacies as tea without bags, fish and chips and candy floss.'

La Manga on the Costa Blanca is described by one tour operator as 'a brilliant new modern resort geared to the contemporary holiday maker'; the gazetteer is not so keen: 'The resort at present comprises a straggling hotch-potch of skyscraper apartment blocks, hotels, clubs of all descriptions, bars, etc.; the whole representing a thoroughly untidy conglomeration.'

Then there's the little town of Porto Christo which one operator claimed had managed to retain 'the character and charm of a fishing village'; but the gazetteer revealed what the brochure discreetly concealed: 'Porto Christo thrives on the daily influx of coach parties who flood the main restaurants, swallow their set menus and scavenge the souvenir shops before "everybody back on the coach again" and the little town is left in peace—until the morrow.'

At a time when eight British tour operators were offering package deals to Cala de Mallorca ('a secluded and relatively unspoiled resort which provides an ideal very relaxing holiday area due to its natural beauty') the gazetteer said: 'The few completed and half-completed hotels stand dispiritedly in an ocean of rock and rubble and what the resort lacks in atmosphere—and shade—it makes up in sheer mess and noise. When the wind blows it can be decidedly invigorating.'

As long as one understands that when a travel brochure talks about a place being 'ideal to relax in' it really means that there is absolutely nothing whatever to *do*, no harm is done. To some people Skegness is 'bracing'; to others it is unpleasantly windy. When truth is *that* relative, one's sympathies go out to the Yorkshire butcher who, accused of raising his meat prices at the weekend, pointed out that, on the contrary he *lowered* them during the week.

Although media men in Britain are beginning to exploit to the full the possibilities of verbal hocus-pocus, they are novices compared with the practitioners in America, a country whose creative use of language leads the world. In a Los Angeles shop window I once saw a vividly horrid painting of what appeared to be a rough sea described as 'an original watercolor reproduction'.

But the most specious use of oxymoron I actually heard came from a television set. 'Stand by', said a portentous voice

12

vibrating with sincerity, 'for a live recording.' I asked my American host what he understood by that announcement.

'Well it's a live recording. A recording actually coming *live* at this moment in time, like *now*.' When you can have 'live recordings', 'loyalty' to a soap powder and 'faith' in a stain remover; when 'style' is attributed to a candy bar, delusion is complete. Perhaps the ultimate confusion—between life and death itself—is the final manifestation of the adman's approach to marketing. If you can package death as an optional extra then surely art can reach no further.

At first glance it might seem that such an idea could only be embraced by the mentally unstable but in Forest Lawn, America's contribution to Man's final gullibility, it reaches its apotheosis. Dr Hubert Eaton, the builder of this first non-necropolis, believed in a happy Eternal Life.

'I therefore prayerfully resolve', he said on New Year's Day 1917, 'that I shall endeavor to build Forest Lawn as different, as unlike other cemeteries as sunshine is unlike darkness, as Eternal Life is unlike Death.'

These great parks are rich in beauty, even richer in prose: 'shrines of memory which not only honor the departed but are also centers of cultural and spiritual service to the living.'

The cadences roll over you like Los Angeles smog. These 'gardens and courts of quiet beauty' symbolise a headlong flight from reality. All is fake. Here larger than life is the Tudor-style Administration Building ('adapted from a famous English Manor House'). Here is the Little Church of the Flowers ('inspired by the ancient church at Stoke Poges'); here the Wee Kirk O' the Heather, a replica of the church where worshipped famed Annie Laurie; there a reproduction of the gracious church of St Margaret in Rottingdean, England—a memorial to the religious poems of the great English poet-novelist Rudyard Kipling.

No expense has been spared to assault the eye. Within Forest Lawn are *all* of Michelangelo's greatest sculptural works in exact reproduction, 'the only place in the world where these may be found together'. There are other masterworks all faithfully reflecting the spirit of the Great Exhibition of 1851. There's a 'kindly Christ surrounded by children, created especially for

13

Forest Lawn by Italian sculptor, Vincenzo Jerace'—although it looks as if it has been executed in cake-icing, this on closer inspection turns out not to be the case.

After a day of wandering I found it difficult to decide which was the most notable vulgarity. Perhaps it was the Memorial Court of Honor described more in hope than accuracy as 'the Westminster Abbey of the New World'. Entombed in this fabrication were such 'Immortals' as Gutzon Norglum, Dr Robert Andrews Millikan, Jan Styka and Rufus B. von Kleinsmid. Had the guide turned out to be Groucho Marx he would not have been noticeably out of place.

Jan Styka, not a name widely known in the world of art, is the perpetrator of a vast photographically vivid painting of Calvary in the manner of Etty. Its only claim to fame is that acre for acre it is the largest religious painting in the world.

There is also an outdoor mosaic in a jumbo-size frame depicting the Ascension, composed of a million pieces of Venetian glass in 3,000 shades of colour. There are other oddities at Forest Lawn, oddities, that is, for a cemetery; a collection of noteworthy gems, all the coins mentioned in the Bible, and a reproduction, carved in ivory, of the Taj Mahal. Forest Lawn reminded me more than a little of Hearst's great palace of San Simeon. Both these manifestations of Californian culture seem to have been created in the belief that More is Better.

Maybe if you've spent a lifetime living in the fantasy world of Beverley Hills or Hollywood it is fitting that the Final Tribute should occur in these Disneyland surroundings, where nothing is what it seems. Indeed, at any moment you half expect the March Hare to scuttle by, or see Alice herself mushrooming bigger even than the truly awful mosaic, 4,950 square feet of it, composed of ten million pieces of glass and depicting the Birth of America.

The Mad Hatter atmosphere of Forest Lawn is so contagious that it has overflowed into the animal kingdom. In the USA a new pet necropolis opens every three months. The oldest and largest, the Imperial Crown Cemetery in the St Louis suburb of Florissant, Mo., contains 7,000 graves of such assorted animals as cats, dogs, parakeets, canaries, rabbits, goldfish and guinea pigs.

The price of a funeral ranges from about $80 to $120 depending on the size of the animal, the type of coffin and the area of the plot.

Mrs Pat Booser, owner of the Paw Print Gardens in West Chicago and founder of the Association of National Pet Cemeteries, has inaugurated a cost-conscious interment for poorer pet-owners. Called a 'country estate burial', it features a hermetically sealed vault which is deposited in a communal grave for $12·50. In some pet cemeteries you may rent the services of a minister of religion to conduct the last rites and speed a dumb friend to the Great Petshop in the Sky. After burial many owners continue to visit the shrine of their defunct pet, perhaps to deposit a bone on the grave of a dog or scatter millet for a budgie. At one period a wealthy American child was flying hundreds of miles every weekend to grieve over the grave of her hamster Beanie.

These anthropomorphic burial grounds for animals are no more or indeed no less surprising than the memorial parks and mortuaries designed for their owners. The death mythology of which they are the outward expression has reached beyond credulity and into an altogether rarified plane of nonsense.

TWO

UP THE GARDEN PATH

You might think that if an Englishman's home is his castle the very worst place to get the better of him would be on his own doorstep; paradoxically it's here that he seems to be at his most gullible. The more preposterous the story the more easily he laps it up; although more often than not it's the lady of the house who is conned, not because she is any thicker than her mate but because she is more likely to answer the door.

When Elizabeth Gundrey, founder-editor of *Shopper's Guide*, wrote her exposé of high-pressure sales methods (*A Foot In The Door*, Frederick Muller, 1965) she listed hundreds of petty swindles and deceits. In the ten years since then the arm of doorstep con-men has grown not only in size but in cunniyng. Some of the small-time operators go to elaborate lengths to make a few pence and one often feels that they'd earn more money with less effort if they took a regular nine-to-five job. One man with a surrealist sense of the ridiculous has set himself up as a catcher of imaginary rats. He knocks on the door, informs you that you have rats in your garden and then in return for a small fee proceeds to fumigate your property and lay out poison.

The most cumbersome trick in recent years is worked by a quartet of small-time dung dealers. They turned up at a house in

17

Eltham in August 1970 and told the woman who lived there that her horse manure had arrived. The woman, who shared the house with her married daughter, assuming that her son-in-law had ordered it allowed the men to carry forty-two bins into the minute back yard. When she suggested to the men that the order was a little large they told her there were another seventy-two bins to come. She gave them £5 to go away.

In the same road another victim parted with £33·50. 'They kept on carrying bins full of the stuff to the back garden', the housewife said, 'and when I asked them to stop they didn't take any notice.' An Eltham police spokesman estimated that she received enough manure to fertilise a five-acre field.

Some dodges would win an award for ingenuity at any international crooks' convention. In Hamburg in the autumn of 1968 two men came round and for a fee the equivalent of £1 bored 4 cm (1½″) diameter holes in the front doors of council houses. They left behind a permanent draught and a large number of council tenants waiting expectantly for the arrival of a glass device which would enable them to 'spot spivs through the door without having to open it'. In Bonn a man called on housewives and sold them pills which he guaranteed would improve their children's school performance in a startling manner. The pills themselves were harmless and useless.

Most cons worked at the door call for a considerable display of acting ability. Take the mother who appears late at night with a feeding bottle in her hand. She is on the verge of tears, the car has broken down: 'Could you possibly warm this milk for me?' A few days later an effusive 'thank-you' letter arrives with a couple of theatre tickets. While the couple are enjoying their evening out the 'mother' returns with an accomplice and ransacks the house.

And the three jolly furniture men are so genuine that their act never fails. You go on holiday and give your front door key to a neighbour. A few days later a delivery van arrives with a large wardrobe. The men ask your neighbour if they can borrow the key. Being a suspicious woman she doesn't give them the key but comes with them. The wardrobe is carried into the hall by the two men and she escorts them out, locking the door behind her. An hour later they arrive back, very apologetic. It wasn't

18

16 Cranford *Gardens* they say but 16 Cranford *Drive*; would she mind very much letting them in to collect it? Again she comes with them, watches them pick up the wardrobe and sees them safely off the premises before locking the front door. The two men have been in the house for less than half a minute and on each occasion supervised by the wary neighbour. What she didn't know was that a third man was concealed in the wardrobe. He had a leisurely hour in which to emerge, clear the house of valuables and lock them and himself back in the wardrobe.

The stage lost a great deal of talent too when an extraordinary band of fast-travelling Scotsmen emigrated to the New World in 1914. Known as The Terrible Williamsons their annual haul is currently estimated at a million dollars. They specialise in re-surfacing drives and general handiwork. When they swept down on Pasadena, California, they were calling themselves 'municipal electrical inspectors'. They would look at your wiring, pronounce it dangerous and recommend that it be replaced by one of the clan. An eighty-six-year-old American once paid some Williamsons $635 for roof-repair work. So gullible did they find him that the following year they came back and did $1,375 more work on the roof and again the following year they deprived him of a further $760. Unfortunately in the fourth year the old man's daughter was in residence and the clan strategically withdrew.

The Williamsons use a variety of names and tell the tale with charm and romance. They commute across the States from Florida to the borders of Canada in brightly painted vans and cars. Since they always perform some kind of service, however sketchy and extortionate, it is difficult to have them charged with fraud. By the time the victim has realised that his yard has been only thinly tarred or his wiring only partially renewed, the Terrible Williamsons have disappeared down the Highway in a cloud of dust and are already double-dealing in a town miles away.

Their womenfolk sell 'antique Irish lace' and 'Scottish woollens'—shoddy goods bought wholesale from some American mill. Usually they suggest to the housewife that if only she will buy the last piece of priceless family lace they will be able to afford an airline ticket back to the peat-wreathed family croft in Scotland. Sobbing from door to door they make as much as the men and leave behind the warm glow which comes to all who have extended a helping hand to the distressed.

Canada and America don't have a monopoly on the large travelling gang. The Williamsons, terrible as they may be, do give some kind of service, however valueless. But a particularly despicable confidence trick was worked in Yorkshire in the late 1960s. It was terminated dramatically in June 1969 when four men were jailed at Northamptonshire Assizes. A gang estimated to number 140 roamed over thirteen counties masquerading as rating officials and inspecting houses with a view to lowering the rates. While one man engaged the occupant in conversation the other, armed with a tape measure, wandered from room to room stealing money and any valuables small enough to be pocketed. The gang specialised in houses occupied by old people living alone, many of whom had bad eyesight and a confused idea of what was happening. The gang often wore false moustaches and dyed their hair to cover their tracks and it took a combined effort over several years before the police could bring them to justice.

The alacrity with which a woman will invite a stranger into her house makes it unnecessary for any potential thief to break and enter. One crook has a foolproof system for giving himself the run of a house. Posing as a 'Man From the Ministry' he asks the housewife if she would be kind enough to stand in the lavatory and hold very firmly onto the ballcock in the cistern. One woman held on for an hour before she got down from the bathroom stool to find both the 'Ministry official' and her jewellery gone.

Then there's the visitor with the Homburg hat, umbrella and large briefcase. Raising his hat he asks in a posh voice whether he can see Madam's birth certificate: 'We have evidence that you may have been left a substantial legacy.' While the excited wife is hunting through the bureau in the sitting room the 'solicitor' is helping himself to the contents of her purse in the kitchen and filling his briefcase with whatever he can lay his hands on.

Sometimes the borderline between robbery with politeness and robbery with violence is very thin. One gang of twenty-five to thirty totters who were terrorising old people in Hampshire and the Isle of Wight stopped just short of actual physical assault. Two or three men would knock at the door of a house and by intimidation force their way in. One eighty-six-year-old widow was persuaded to part with a painting worth at least £1,000 for only £26·50. Another old woman was asked to 'admire' the gold rings on a caller's hand—they looked more like knuckledusters to her. To keep within the letter of the law a receipt was always left, money always handed over, but the visits were usually an occasion for extortion.

Sometimes a wave of mass hysteria will overwhelm a whole street of housewives and they will start buying expensive consumer durables as if possessed by some kind of demon. In June 1970 in the village of Berinsfield in Oxfordshire, eighty-four housewives agreed to pay £306 each over five years for deepfreezers which they could have bought at the local electricity showroom for £94. Many cottages were so small that the only place big enough to install the giant 14·3-cubic-foot freezer was the living room, where it dwarfed everything and presumably every few minutes burst into a merry and cripplingly expensive electric hum.

Often the patter of a doorstep salesman is so fast and convincing that the victim is mesmerised into signing on the dotted line for washing machines, central heating, vacuum cleaners and magazines. Two youngsters in their early twenties collected almost £2,000 from villagers in Yorkshire. They sold subscriptions to magazines and told their victims that the magazines would not begin to arrive until 120 days had elapsed. How they were able to con subscriptions in January for magazines which wouldn't arrive until May, if at all, is anybody's guess. They were jailed for a year in 1970.

'I'm from the Press,' said a well-dressed man who forced his way into my kitchen a few years ago. He turned out to be not from *The Times* or even the *Putney and Roehampton Herald Incorporating The Sheen Gazette and Barnes Advertiser*, but from, he alleged, Odhams Press and he was peddling a set of encyclopaedias without which none of my children would ever be able to pass an exam. If I failed to sign on the dotted line I would be consigning the boy to destitution in a blacking factory and the girl to a lifetime of drudgery. 'You can't afford not to have these books in your home,' he said. I could just imagine how convincing his pitch would be in a household where the only book around was the *Family Doctor and Handy Home Mechanic*.

'I'm from the Education Department. . . . I've come about your child's future. . . . I'm conducting a survey for an educational foundation. . . . I'm trying to work my way through college. . . . I'm from the Parent-Pupil Development Programme. . . .' All these are opening gambits in a spiel which may leave you committed to pay sometimes as much as £200 for a set of encyclopaedias.

The monstrous regiment of thieves and mountebanks dedicated to charming away your money and property grows daily. Spurious collectors, rag-and-bone men, gipsies, knifegrinders, market researchers, medicine men, beggars, deaf-aid repair men, carpet sellers, Indian bagmen, penniless artists . . . you need never be alone. This huge stage army of mendicants seldom knock in vain, however unlikely their story. In Basildon in September 1970 a man in his mid-thirties with brown wavy hair posed as a doctor and persuaded housewives to allow him to undress them. They all stripped without protest when he announced that he was seeking a cholera contact from the Middle East.

I'm convinced that if a man in a bowler hat turned up and said that he was from the Council and that he was going to have to remove all your silver, jewellery, clocks, radio and TV set to an underground laboratory to be checked for radiation as a lorry containing uranium had overturned in the High Street during the night the average housewife would hand over the lot.

Who, for instance, could resist this appeal which was shoved through my letter box recently: 'The Lord said: "Seek not your reward on this earth but in the Kingdom of God".' 'DISABLED EX-SERVICEMEN'S COLLECTION . . . Dear Friends: Has it been your misfortune to have someone dear to you disabled by their services—through the war, or perhaps you know somebody in this most unhappy position, then if so, you can quite understand their predicament in trying to get regular employment: Hence your support trusting you will try and be a good Christian in this worthy cause.' This fairly breathless appeal then went on to ask me to turn out my attic: 'Anything that you may have to dispose of will be greatly appreciated: sewing machines, domestic appliances, musical instruments, old ornaments, china and glassware. . . .' The list was comprehensive. 'This is not a charitable appeal,' the letter said, 'a fee will be paid to you for whatever you have to dispose of.' When I rang the telephone number in the East End of London from which this enterprise was directed, the man who was running it revealed that he was not disabled but he had a brother who was. 'Don't pick on me, mate,' he said, 'there's lots of us at it.'

Another morning a man in his fifties came to the door wearing the kind of dark glasses usually associated with impaired sight. He was selling furniture polish to help ex-Servicemen. Being an ex-Serviceman myself, as indeed the majority of my generation are, I asked him in what way I was about to be helped: 'Well,' he said, 'it's for ex-Servicemen in general, you know, people like me.' There was nothing wrong with his eyes only they tended to water a bit in sunlight, he said. Being hard-hearted and ruthless I refused the chance to buy his grossly overpriced polish. But very few housewives, many of whom might have lost relatives either in the First or Second World War, could have withstood such a direct assault on their sense of patriotism.

Flannels for ex-Servicemen, soap for the blind, lace handkerchiefs to help orphans, combs to ease the lot of the handicapped, all are irresistible doorstep appeals. But it's when the housewife ventures down the garden path and hares off to the High Street that her defences seem finally to crumble. Most women assume that they have some innate gift which makes them wise and careful shoppers. But the very opposite is the case. Modern merchandising takes full advantage of our natural naivety and our inability to work out even the simplest price equation. With great skill the marketing men make a simple comparison of values almost impossible without enlisting the aid of a computer.

There's a semantic sleight of hand which makes even the size of a packet open to dispute. Words like *Giant, Jumbo, Super, Economy, Budget, Household, Special,* when used quantitatively

B

have long ceased to have any other than an emotive meaning. The big cardboard packet of corn flakes when opened is found to be far from full, and who knows the true price of an article which is packaged with a free sachet of shampoo, 2p off, treble stamps and a voucher entitling you to enter a competition for a two-week African safari?

To navigate successfully through the aisles of a really profit-oriented supermarket requires an almost professional skill. From the moment that the shopper is enticed inside by a specious offer of baked beans below cost price or a smashing reduction on tinned pears, she is at the mercy of supersalesmanship which has been programmed by psychologists and men whose only concern is to shift merchandise. Very often something that every housewife needs (flour for instance) is placed at ground level. She bends down to get it and as she straightens up there facing her at eye-level is a tin of expensive salmon or a convenience dinner—on impulse she takes one. Every housewife needs meat, so the meat is placed right at the back of the store. To reach it she has to make two journeys up and down the whole length of the shelves. Lighting is planned to make food tempting—meat and bacon look more luscious in a pinky-red glow so that's the way the lights are fixed. Everywhere the housewife looks she sees an abundance of tins. Great mountains of canned fruit or beans remind her how empty her larder is. Psychologists have found that a shopper doesn't like to disturb a symmetrically arranged pyramid of packaged goods so the cans are thrown at random into enormous baskets. 'There is plenty for everyone, help yourself', they seem to say.

Very often the loss leader (THIS WEEK'S BONANZA BARGAIN TWO POUNDS OF SUGAR FOR ONLY 7P) will be hidden away in some obscure corner of the store so that before a woman finds it she has seen and fallen prey to a variety of goods she had no intention of buying and which are not quite the bargains that the sugar is.

Even the huge shopping trolleys themselves are an invitation to be a big spender. Several times the size of the ordinary shopping basket, they swallow up the goodies and even when full are easy to push about—the shopper is never made to feel aware of the weight of the goods she has grabbed. The toys at child's eye-level, the tempting sweets stacked at the checkouts are all there for a calculated and clinical purpose. As one supermarket executive told me: 'Con? Well, we're in the business of selling aren't we and it's up to us to move the produce. It's commonsense to put tins of cream next to tins of fruit. You've got to keep nudging people, reminding them what they want.' And what they *don't* want? 'Well if they didn't want it they wouldn't buy it would they? They're not children you know, they're supposed to be sensible mature adults.'

Shopping for toothpaste or shopping for cars means taking a great deal on trust. The average citizen confronted with a complicated piece of electronic equipment can only take the salesman's word that it will live up to the claims made for it in the advertisements. Presumably if you're buying a Rolls-Royce for £14,000 everything might be expected to be of the best. But for the driver who can't afford that sort of luxury even buying a car has become a calculated risk. Who do you believe? Ralph Nader, who says the car you're buying is unsafe and potentially lethal, or the company which claims it embodies every safety device known to technology?

Only when you've bought a car do you begin to become aware of what you've let yourself in for. Every time a campaigning newspaper enquires into the state of the car industry a storm of discontent is unleashed in the correspondence columns. Readers vie to produce tall stories from their garage of memories. Cars with faultily assembled gudgeon cranks, cars with no gudgeon cranks at all. New cars that were found by some independent observer to have thirty-nine faults and cars that had to be taken back time and again for repair.

Having anything repaired is in many instances an open invitation for the unscrupulous to exercise their imagination. When a watch stops or a television set breaks down the ordinary person places himself completely in the hands of the expert. What can happen then has been affording a field day for both Press and TV for several years. Perhaps the most hilarious evening's viewing in Britain came from Granada's 'World in Action' team. They bought a brand new television receiver, severed the aerial lead where it joins the socket, sprayed it with dust to make it look used and then took it to be repaired. The first shop reconnected the lead and charged for replacing a valve—they were not able to hand back the original brand new valve because it had been 'thrown out'. Total charge £2·51. The second shop reconnected the lead, found a non-existent fault in the printed circuit and charged £1·50. The third shop didn't repair the fault but claimed they'd replaced a valve, handed back an old valve not fitted in the set in the first place and asked for £3. The fourth shop reconnected the lead, supplied two new valves, handed back two old valves which had not come from the set and charged £4·75.

Even more arbitrary were the antics of the watch repair men. The Granada team bought four new watches and got a technician in a watch laboratory to put them out of action by removing a screw and leaving it in the case. The first repairer put the screw back on the spot and charged 25p, another shop charged 47½p and took two days, a third shop took two weeks and charged £1·50 and a large firm took ten days and attached a bill for £2·50. As Mr Frank West, secretary of the British Horological Institute, said at the time: 'Any member of the public can go out, purchase himself a shop and set himself up as a watchmaker and jeweller.' *Caveat emptor*.

And let the buyer beware wherever he goes. Let him beware of the London or Birmingham greengrocer who takes his leftover fruit and vegetables out into the country at the weekend and sets up a stall on a verge. The Sunday motorists stop to buy what they assume will be fresh-picked strawberries and tender young peas at bargain prices. But more often than not the prices are 25 per cent higher than they were in the shop the day before.

Let the buyer beware too of the fantastic and incredible shopping bargains that besprinkle the pages of the weekend papers. There seems to be a theory in advertising circles that on Saturday and Sunday everyone's resistance reaches a paralysing ebb. All week the papers are advertising sensible things like computer systems and cough mixture but come Saturday the pages are flooded with offers for articles which you would not normally imagine you might need: silver-plated butter curlers, buoyant foam bed wedges, hip cycles, distance-defeating binoculars, heat-resistant doilies, egg scissors and magic manual hole borers.

Magic is a key word on the postal bargain pages—all stitchers are magic or miracle, so you can have a miracle three-in-one oil (use it on your bike, tasty in salads too).

There's an emphasis on speed: Rush me your handcrafted fit-on-the-knee portable desk top indispensable for the housewife and author! Rush me your giant four-inch-high Regency-type Bohemian glass chandelier which will add lustre to my lounge! Rush me too your glorious shrub rose hedging to ring my garden with fabulously perfumed living colour and while you're at it rush me your incredible new scientific device which will minimise tension, reduce eyestrain and fatigue and cut my corns in half the time!

Time is a great obsession, as if the people who read Saturday's papers haven't got a moment to lose. Things trim in a minute, sew in a jiffy, cook while-u-wait, remove unwanted blemishes in a second. There are frequent specious claims of 55 per cent reductions and vague suggestions that the advertiser ought to be under psychiatric observation: 'LATEST MAD MAD MAD OFFER . . . UNDER HALF THE PRICE WE COULD CHARGE.'

There's also a naïve assumption that Saturday is the one day of the week when the halt and the maimed buy a paper. There are scores of advertisements for all-purpose backrests, rupture appliances, step-in corselettes, wonder salts, miracle bunion cures, collapsible commodes and constructions to take the weight of bedclothes off your ankles.

It's a world of unique luxury envelope offers, astonishing crocus reductions and daring peek-a-boo see-through nightie-negligees.

I think the Advertising Association ought to award an annual prize (perhaps a size 15 ex-ARP Warden's heavy duty wellie) for the most baroque article of the year. I don't mean anything mundane like 5,000 miles of substandard telephone cable suitable for tying up raspberry canes, or a plastic cakestand on wheels, but something really creative. A propelling pen with eighteen different colour inks and the Lord's Prayer engraved on the nib might fill the bill, or a fantastic multi-purpose implement that could cut your hair, stone cherries, ease tired limbs, hang wallpaper in a trice, polish the car and banish arthritis overnight. It would have to be unique and revolutionary and surplus to requirements and fantastic value—and of course utterly and totally useless.

THREE

FAIRIES AT THE BOTTOM OF THE BOTTLE

There is nothing in which man is more intimately interested than his health. When we are ravaged by illness, reason flies out of the window; we are as vulnerable as patients etherised upon a table, ripe for any suggestion, however unorthodox, however desperate.

In Britain if you have a sore throat a chemist will more than likely give you a heavily advertised something to pour down it. In Italy, as I once found to my surprise, (was *strozza* the right word or had I confused it with some more fundamental part of the anatomy?) they will paradoxically offer you a suppository. Allopathy, acupuncture, psychotherapy, herbalism, osteopathy, yoga, hypnotherapy, radiesthesia, faith healing, homoeopathy, auto-suggestion, naturopathy, and chiropractic are among the more widespread alternative treatments which you might try if establishment techniques aren't doing much good. And if those fail there's always a lucky rabbit's paw. One might imagine from the confidence that some people have in self-medication that they are expertly acquainted with the working of their own body. But our ignorance is frightening. In 1971 Dr P. Ley told the psychology section of the British Association about a survey which had been conducted in Glasgow. It revealed that 48 per cent of those questioned did not know where their heart was; 49 per cent their lungs; 52 per cent their intestines; 57 per cent their kidneys and 80 per cent their stomachs. Another test showed that 37 per cent of patients forgot what the doctor had told them within ten minutes and 41 per cent forgot in eighty minutes. With such a high degree of ignorance you might reasonably expect the sick to throw themselves without reserve on the mercy of a doctor, but there still remains a universal and perhaps well-founded suspicion of professional treatment; many people feel instinctively with George Bernard Shaw that 'all professions are conspiracies against the laity'. This is why it is a common sight to see normally sensible adults discussing their symptoms earnestly in the chemist's with a young girl fresh from school but dressed in a hygienic and helpful-looking white coat—the sort of therapeutic garment affected by eminent surgeons, garage foremen and other figures of authority. A common sight too, in the few market places left by the developers, to see a crowd standing mesmerised by a patent medicine salesman. 'I'm not here for my health,' I heard a market quack announce not very long ago, 'I am here for yours.' The patter that followed was straight out of the eighteenth century and it held a Lancashire crowd spellbound. It was difficult to believe that this was 1974 and not 1774. The man wore a Homburg hat and half-glasses. Although the accent was basically northern, among the fallen h's there were slight overtones of Harley Street:

It is a wet day my friends and I have a busy schedule; I come among you for one purpose and one purpose only—to allow you the same treatment that is now being prescribed for a very few in high places. Princess Anne, members of the jet set, Aristotle Onassis, Princess Grace of Monte Carlo, His Royal Highness the Aga Khan, the Maharishi. They are paying thousands of guineas for a treatment which to you, my dear good friends, is a matter of pence.

This is a potion used exclusively by Harley Street consultants, a potion that can be procured only with the greatest difficulty due to financial restrictions and currency

regulations. This is not a medicine, not a painkiller, it is as it says a Universal Balm. It will cure arthritis, neuritis, neuralgia, old-algia *(laughter)*, any algia you've got. Aches and pains of all kinds succumb to its lightning action. It sweeps as it cleans *(laughter)*. Just follow the simple instructions, a teaspoonful before retiring in your milk or Guinness *(laughter)* and Bob's your uncle. If you're run down, bunged-up *(shrieks of mock modesty)* or just plain fed up try this. Even if it does you no good it can't do you any harm. I am not asking a hundred pounds nor a pound, nor fifty pence. . . .

Totally in defiance of the Trade Descriptions Act, and no doubt in defiance of every drug regulation in the book, the bottles quickly emptied from the suitcase and as quickly as he had arrived the Medicine Man was gone. As Shaw noted in *The Doctor's Dilemma*:

> Belief can be produced in practically unlimited quantity and intensity without observation or reasoning, and even in defiance of both by the simple desire to believe founded on a strong interest in believing. It is this naive credulity coupled with a desire to be relieved of pain at whatever cost and in whatever eccentric way that medical mountebanks have always thrived upon.

Three hundred years ago a con man called Edmund Buckworth was selling five-shilling bags which if hung round a child's neck not only prevented but even cured rickets. Two hundred years ago you could buy a salve to anoint the tongue and cure stammering, an electuary which would revive thought, judgment, apprehension, reason and memory at only 2s 6d a pot, and Samuel Major was peddling from his headquarters near Half-Moon Alley in Bishopsgate snuff which would cure the mentally deranged and 'all Disorders of Body and Mind'.

A hundred years ago there were anti-pain plasters which cured weak lungs in one minute, electropathic belts that banished paralysis, indigestion and epilepsy and electric garters which improved ill-shapen and dwarfed limbs. The nineteenth century was rich in gadgets and medicines which could cure everything at one go including fallen arches and damp in the cellar. In 1908 the British Medical Association estimated that the public was spending £2,500,000 a year on secret remedies—enough, as they said, to maintain 40,000 hospital beds. Stamp duty alone from this national confidence trick netted £334,142. Not content with inventing non-cures for real diseases the quacks peddled non-cures for non-diseases such as 'brain fag', 'tobacco heart', 'tired voice', 'catarrh of the bowels' and 'shopper's headache'. The majority of the remedies were surrounded with a veil of secrecy. The BMA published a chemical analysis of the more common medicines and it turned out that the ingredients of the pills and ointments and fluids were often as cheap as they were nasty. Munyon's Blood Cure, manufactured in America ('It eradicates all Impurities from the Blood, and cures Scrofulitic Eruptions, Rash on the Scalp, Itching and Burning, and any form of Unhealthy, Blotchy, Pimply or Scaly Skin') contained nothing but sugar. The estimated cost of these pills was one-thirtieth of a penny, the price, *one shilling*.

It's hard to see how the BMA kept a straight face as they went about their task. The names of the remedies were sometimes as preposterous as their ingredients: Mother Seigel's Curative Syrup, Keene's One Night Cold Cure, The Brompton Consumption and Cough Specific, Trench's Remedy for Epilepsy and Fits, Alfred Crompton's Specific for Deafness, The Teetolia Treatment, Dr Martin's Miracletts, Antidipso, Antigout Soap, Bell's Fairy Cure, Bishop's Gout Varalettes, Pesqui's Uranium Wine, even Pink Pills for Pale People.

The BMA's researches were naturally given little publicity in those papers which derived a substantial part of their revenue from advertising bogus cures for cancer, diabetes and tuberculosis. As *John Bull*, under the editorship of the notable swindler Horatio Bottomley, trumpeted:

The formulae of patent medicines are compounded by chemists at least as well qualified as those who dispense the undisclosed formulae of medical practitioners, and any legislative action which would harass, obstruct, or prohibit their sale would not only be a grave injustice to them, but a wholly unwarrantable interference with the right of the public to doctor itself as it pleases.

It is difficult to believe that any journalist who had read *Secret Remedies* (by 1909 it had sold 114,000 copies) could make such a claim. The BMA had proved beyond a shadow of suspicion that the majority of patent medicines on sale were unpleasant, unnecessarily expensive and almost totally useless. 'It is not', the BMA noted, 'only the poorer classes of the community who have a weakness for secret remedies and the ministrations of quacks; the well-to-do and highly placed will often, when not very ill, take a curious pleasure in experimenting with mysterious compounds.'

But *John Bull* was right, the public has always regarded itself as having an inalienable right to doctor itself. Although Parliament is still labouring to protect us from ourselves, no amount of legislation seems able to diminish our irresponsibility; we are still prepared to swallow anything as long as the claims are sufficiently preposterous.

In more credulous times it was thought that a substance would one day be discovered which would be able to prolong life indefinitely. Elixirs are still in demand especially among people who have some indefinable feeling of not being as well as they might. One of the many products marketed for those who need bucking up is Bio-Strath.

Something approaching three-quarters of a million bottles of Bio-Strath Elixir are sold in Britain alone every year; it costs just under £1·50 a bottle which puts it in the luxury class, but of course when you are buying an elixir, money has no meaning. When the Consumers' Association investigated the claims of Bio-Strath in 1970 they were unimpressed. Well-known figures bursting with health and vitality are used to attest the virtues of the product, which is alleged to be made by feeding yeast with over ninety 'medicinal herbs' and then adding germinated barley, honey and the juice from 'biologically grown apples'. What it doesn't say anywhere on the bottle or in the advertising is that Bio-Strath is as alcoholic as beer. On the box in which the Swiss elixir is packed there's a formidable list of enzymes, vitamins,

34

minerals and amino acids. Somewhat ungraciously the CA evaluated these portentous ingredients. Enzymes, they said, were of no special value since they are broken down before being taken up by the body. Cheese they thought gave you ten times as many amino acids, ounce for ounce, as Bio-Strath and they found that there was about five times as much vitamin C in one lowly potato chip as in the daily dose of Bio-Strath. As for the specific claim that the product gave you energy, they revealed that a cup of sweetened tea would give you a similar calorific value. Their conclusion on the value of Bio-Strath: 'It all depends whether you think there are fairies at the bottom of the bottle.'

Then there's the monstrous regiment of 'vitamin' pills that are consumed annually in the western world. Few people are vitamin deficient, and since the body can only absorb a certain amount, overdosing with vitamins is a well attested waste of money and can be potentially dangerous. So too with 'tonics', few of which can have any noticeable physiological effect. Tonic wines, apart from costing twice as much as comparable table wines, and often tasting twice as nasty (jam with added iron filings), have little effect beyond making you drunk if you can force enough between your lips.

There are all manner of products designed to brace, fortify, invigorate, strengthen the nerves and pick you up, and many of them contain iron. The association of iron ('his nerves were of iron') with strength is an obvious one. But ingesting excessive quantities of iron is not likely to turn a weakling into a Samson. It's interesting to note that when Sanatogen were looking for new ways in which to promote their tonic wine sales they marketed a brand 'with added iron'. One glass three times a day is claimed to provide your normal daily requirements of iron. As most healthy people get enough iron in their ordinary diet perhaps Sanatogen may be regarded as a non-essential luxury.

Of course there are other ways of getting iron. From Phyllosan for instance, which 'fortifies the over forties'. But the old-established brand leader when it comes to getting your iron rations is Iron Jelloids. 'When blood lacks iron', runs the advertisement, 'it spreads weariness through your body. Life drags, and you don't seem to enjoy *anything*. That's what doctors call simple anaemia, caused by iron deficiency. And there's a simple answer. Iron Jelloids.'

When the CA investigated iron preparations they thought there was a better answer. It was so fundamental that they put it in capitals—'SEE YOUR DOCTOR; anaemia is not a condition you can diagnose or manage yourself.' Weariness, they explained, could be due to causes other than iron deficiency and going to the chemists for Iron Jelloids is likely to delay diagnosis of what may be a serious condition. They were disturbed that nowhere on the leaflet was there a suggestion that if the symptoms persisted a doctor should be consulted.

A word even more magical than iron is phosphorus. It has had a long and inventive medical history. In Victorian times, for instance, there was a product available called Anti-Catarrh. Although it was 74 per cent sugar and only contained 0·07 per cent phosphoric acid the manufacturer made great play with The Wonders of Phosphorus: 'Free (or unoxidised) Phosphorus, whose chief seat or situation is in the brain, is one of the most important elements contained in our bodies. Without Free Phosphorus there can be no thought, and very probably no life. . . .' If it were that important you might wonder why Mr Birley only provided 0·07 parts of such a fundamental mineral: 'One thing is proved beyond doubt, that the degree of intellectual thought depends upon the amount of Free Phosphorus in the brain, and just as the Phosphorus is unduly wasted, so does the brain power weaken. . . .'

Of course we know better today. Or do we? Phosphorus compounds are still a favoured ingredient of nerve foods and tonic wines: sodium glycerophosphate, dilute phosphoric and glycerophosphoric acid all make their appearance on the labels and one tonic, Phospherine, has an eponymous name. The theory is that since there is phosphorus in the brain and the nerves, the more phosphorus you ingest the better your brain and nerves will function. In his book *The Drugs You Take* (Pan Books, 1968), Dr S. Bradshaw claimed that the phosphorus lark was 'just about the biggest bit of nonsense in the whole tonic field'. As far as doctors are concerned, he wrote, 'no one has ever been shown to be ill as a result of shortages of phosphorus . . . when taken by mouth, glycerophosphates are broken down in one's digestive system; in other words they cannot even reach one's nerve tissue . . . the best one can say about them is that they're harmless to the body, if not the purse.'

The British also set great store by salts—'Wonderful', they cry, 'good as a dose of salts.' Many of the six million people in Britain who suffer from rheumatic diseases pin their faith in 'salts', the most popular being Kruschen Salts, Juno Junipah Mineral Salts and Fynnon Salt. The first of these is mainly magnesium sulphate (Epsom Salts) and the other two are mainly sodium sulphate (Glauber's Salts). When the ungullible CA investigated these three remedies, it pointed out that they were laxatives. They thought it wrong that laxatives should be advertised for the relief of rheumatic pain. As with all self-medication their message was clear: 'If you have persistent aches and pains you must see a doctor. If you take one of these rheumatic salts instead, you are depriving yourself of the best treatment available to ease your pain.'

A salt far more common than magnesium sulphate or sodium sulphate was being widely sold in the north of England in 1970. It was claimed to be 'particularly beneficial for the treatment and alleviation of all maladies common to the feet'. Called Pedabrine, it cost about 75p a hundredweight and was being sold for 30p a pound. It was no more than a cleaned-up version of the rock salt that workmen strew on icy roads. A similar product, under the name of Na-Sal was being sold in Lancashire markets. This was said to alleviate arthritis and rheumatism but on analysis also turned out to be common salt crystals.

Then there's the magic of the magnet. A belief in the beneficial effects of magnetism descends from the sixteenth-century Swiss physician Theophrastus Bombastus von Hohenheim, better known as Paracelsus. He was the first to attribute occult and miraculous powers to the lodestone and his theories are still alive and thriving in the 1970s. Newspapers all over the country regularly advertise Rumaton (£2·95 plus 15p postage) for those who put their faith in copper bracelets. 'If you think copper bracelets are wonderful', claims a long-running advertisement in the national Press, 'wait till you've tried

Rumaton, the new magnetic bracelets. They are terrific! Worn by millions of delighted users! Don't take our word for it—convince yourself.' Rumaton is described as an elegant golden bracelet with six built-in magnets but there is no mention of what precise benefits it will bring you.

Half the battle in marketing a proprietary panacea lies in selecting a potent name—Rumaton, with its association with rheumatism is a good try. And it occurs to me that any drug house wanting to cut themselves a slice of the cold-flu-headache cake might do worse than market some pills under the name of Paracelsus. As the active ingredient will probably be paracetamol the 'para' root is relevant; it also has evocative associations with such words as *para*mount, incom*para*ble, *para*gon, *para*dise and un*para*lleled. The 'celsus' of course has the advantages of bringing to mind such words as *excelsior* and *excellent*, and has an academically authentic Latin ring. The copy almost writes itself:

Feeling run down, nervy, irritable?
Is everything suddenly getting too much for you?
When iron and phosphorus fail, when the salts let you down PARACELSUS does the trick.
Do you tire easily, wake up feeling whacked?
Does the slightest noise set your teeth on edge?
Do you rattle, wheeze, groan and sigh?
Get PARACELSUS the wonder drug or send now for your free one-day trial pack.
Eases pain instantly, removes corns in days.
Pleasant-tasting, faster and more effective relief from everything.
Soon you will feel confident, relaxed, enjoying life to the full like Mrs S. G. Smith of Welwyn Garden City who writes:
'I'm feeling my old self again. . . . I would spend my last penny on Paracelsus.'
Don't forget all the ingredients in Paracelsus are approved by doctors.
Only £1·50 at your chemists—enough for a full seven-day lightning course.

Selling many of today's remedies requires creative literary skill of a high order, but to market brine as a cure-all is perhaps the height of artistry. In February 1968 it became known that the Agency for International Development had expended £10,000 on sea water. It arrived in convincingly labelled tubes under such names as Bioceane and L'Eau de Mer. There was no deception, it was exactly what it said—sea water. Bottled off a beach in Puerto Rico the AID were told vaguely that 'its salty aspects provide some beneficial value against nausea, skin eruption and *other things*'.

Man is at his most gullible when he is contemplating his reproductive powers. He is besieged with worries about whether he is getting enough, could he get more, could it conceivably be better? To pander to these feelings of doubt and inadequacy sex shops have sprung up selling high-priced concoctions to enhance sexual happiness for men as well as women. There are creams to 'maintain a naturally firm and beautiful bosom', creams to 'increase the "swelling capacity" of the penis' and other sexual specifics.

In May 1971 *World Medicine* published a report on some of these products which had been analysed for them by a pharmacologist, Professor Desmond Laurence of University College Hospital. He found that S.K. Dragees (retailed in London at £1·38 for thirty) contained cocoa, coffee, caffeine, and milk powder and were about as aphrodisiac as 'a cup of coffee with milk'. Yet these sweets, manufactured in Western Germany, were claimed to be 'fast acting energy pills' which would bring 'renewed verve and vitality'.

An ointment he examined which was called Antipraecox, was supposed to 'decrease bodily sensitivity to friction, thereby extending the duration of erection and postponing the point of discharge'. At 95p this product (Benzocaine ointment) seemed to the Professor to be an expensive way of buying a local anaesthetic. He analysed another aphrodisiac called Arauna Forte, described as 'a new sexual strengthening agent' whose effect was based on 'known sex strengthening constituents'. These on analysis turned out to be liquid extract of hops, dandelion, St John's wort, lovage root, gentian, ginseng, balm, mistletoe, hawthorn hips and millifollii. The Professor's comment: 'Pending publication of the evidence on which the ingredients are "known" to be "sex strengthening" I would class this as traditional "if you believe that you'll believe anything" type of medicine.'

Another product claimed that it contained hormones which would quickly strengthen 'the *organism*'. Analysis revealed no hormones although the presence of vitamin C and wine might have given your organism, whatever that is, a *frisson*. Professor Laurence found all these products an affront to medical scientific reason. He noted that some of his students had eaten most of the Dragees and drunk most of the Arauna Forte: 'I have not followed them up as the conditions were uncontrolled, but no rumours of unusual behaviour have reached me.'

Miss Ann Summers, who founded the first sex supermarket in Britain to sell these goods, resigned from the company in the following month. Apart from her sex ointments and creams Miss Summers had catered for all tastes. Much in demand were art volumes ('seventy beautiful girls and three vigorous men'), Dinky Baby Doll nighties, sexy soap, sexual massagers, appliances and erotica of all sorts. On resigning from the company Miss Summers pointed out that in her nine months of trading 'thousands of the public have supported my strong belief in the real need for a service of this kind'.

Commenting on the statement, which he described as 'a skilful mingling of pomposity and humbug', Peter Simple in the *Daily Telegraph* noted: 'In a quiet way there is nothing so funny as the pretence that to discover or exploit some new way of making money out of human weakness and gullibility is really to provide a public service.'

After sex, the most obsessional contemporary phobia centres round obesity. In 1971 the mania for slimming by eating bananas or hardboiled eggs gave way (much to the delight of Israel, Cyprus and South Africa) to the grapefruit. The craze was imported from America. Somebody had decided that grapefruit was a catalyst which would start a fat-burning process. According to one of Britain's leading authorities on nutrition, Professor John Yudkin of London University, 'if you waggled your left toe three times on alternate Thursdays it would have exactly the same effect as grapefruit—nothing'.

The grapefruit-eating craze sent the price soaring, and thousands of people mailed £1 each to an American and his wife for the secret of the diet. The diet was published free in most papers but presumably people thought that for £1 they would get even better advice. The advice was quite sound, apart from the description of grapefruit as a catalyst. It advised you to cut down on carbohydrates.

The market was soon flooded with special 'slimming' foods, exercisers ('Now you can get your exercise while reading or watching television') and health clinics ('Lose up to eight inches in one visit').

Over the years the Consumers' Association tested and evaluated a whole series of expensive devices which they invariably found were no substitute for the cheap and simple remedy of eating less. Their advice, based on medical opinion, was simple but seemingly unacceptable: 'We believe that the long-term solution to problems of overweight must be re-forming one's habits permanently by eating much less carbohydrate.' But a Britain used to compulsive eating between meals and a heavy consumption of sweets, buns, chips, cakes and crisps preferred to imagine it could continue to gorge and still grow thin.

While half the population seemed to be trying to reduce their intake of calories the other half were trying to give up smoking. Some of the devices marketed to help them were as ingenious as anything the Victorians could have invented. One of these ('Make Your Lungs A Clean Air Zone') allowed you to smoke your normal quota of cigarettes but they were to be inserted in a 'remarkable cigarette holder created by a team of top Italian scientists'. Surestop, as it was called, worked on the principle of mixing fresh air with the smoke you drew in: 'Week by week you alter the holder so that you inhale less of the harmful smoke and more of the fresh air.'

It reminded me of my still unpatented drink holder for incipient alcoholics. 'Blotto' works on the principle of imbibing your drink through a remarkable beaker created by a team of Venetian glass boffins. Week by week you alter a valve on the

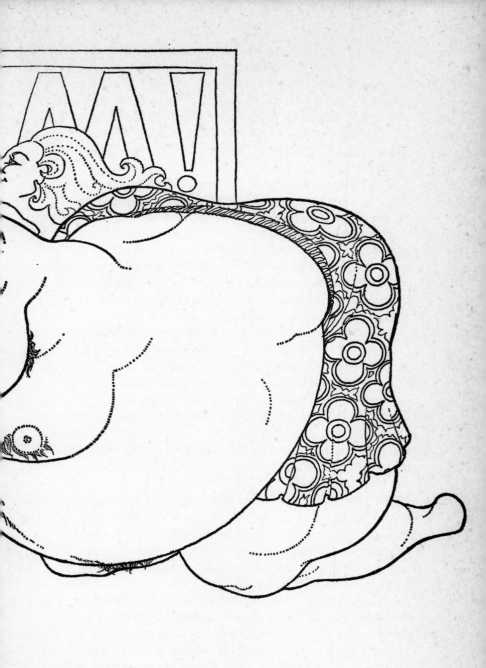

glass so that you swallow less of the harmful alcohol and more fresh tapwater. After about six weeks, just as the advertisement for Surestop says, 'you will have overcome your addiction—painlessly, effectively and with none of the usual WITHDRAWAL AGONIES.' You are left knocking back glass after glass of healthgiving tapwater—and if that becomes boring you can always buy a Surestop cigarette holder for £1·50 and inhale fresh air through it.

Worries about sex, about overweight, about smoking and drinking too much, inevitably lead to a state of widespread unease which the patent medicine men are only too willing to relieve. Most people, if they think about it, are 'nervy', 'irritable' and 'at a low ebb'. Most people tire easily, need a holiday, feel run down or strung up. Most people too have vague aches and coughs and twinges and sharp sudden stabbing pains, even if it's only in the big toe. They are a particular target for the over-anxious patent medicine industry.

One tablet-maker directs his advertisements at those who think they might be suffering from Summer Chestiness. 'There's lots of "Summer Chestiness" about,' the ads read. 'Middle-aged and elderly people particularly get a sense of Bronchial Congestion, feel short of breath and are inclined to "wheeze" and "rattle".' You might think that if anyone was inclined to wheeze and rattle they would ring immediately for an ambulance rather than send a stamped postcard for a twenty-four hour supply of the wonder tablets. But the regular appearance of the advertisements suggests that business is brisk.

Apart from cure-alls for specific complaints, millions of pounds every year are spent on products in which individuals set their own talismanic faith: dried herbs, charcoal biscuits, strange essences and tinctures, tisanes and salves. Then there is the wearing of amulets, medallions, lucky stones and Cornish piskies to ward off diseases.

Even African juju has been known to help the British housewife. In April 1969 an engineer went from Southborne, near Portsmouth, on a business trip to Ghana. He brought back with him a carved figure from the Ashanti area. His wife placed it on the bedroom dressing-table and within three months she had conceived. The doll was lent to a nineteen-year-old girl who had been trying unsuccessfully to become pregnant for six months. Within two weeks she was also expecting. Strange to relate, yet another neighbour borrowed the doll for her dressing-table and within two weeks she also had become pregnant. 'I do believe there is something special about the doll', said one of the women. 'I definitely won't have it upstairs again.'

Although we are protected by legislation from such specifics as Fitch's Kidney and Liver Cooler or Baring Gould's Anti-Rheumatic Pearls there are plenty of fads and fallacies to take their place. If we can't get the jujubes, we'll settle for juju.

FOUR

A FAITH IN HEALING or SEEING IS BELIEVING

Americans have a very engaging habit of over-selling the virtues of their friends and acquaintances, sometimes to such an extent that when you meet these people, or reach, as one might say in the States, a condition of interfacial involvement, it's something of an anticlimax.

'These are darling people', an American host said to me once as we drove into the Blue Mountains to meet a couple who had invited us for lunch.

'Dodie is a saint', my hostess said, 'a living doll!'

'Oh she *is*; a very *human* being.'

'They're just the loveliest couple. Joe just worships the ground she walks on and they have two fine and wonderful children and this very gracious home on a lake.'

The testimonials continued for several miles of Highway and I felt as if I were being taken to meet some latter-day Holy Family. When we arrived at the Sandowskis' they turned out to be ordinary pleasant people, no happier nor more miserable than most middle-class American couples. When Joe, slightly confused by his own jumbo martinis, dropped Dodie's orange chiffon pie on the patio, Dodie let herself go dramatically, but it was fairly obvious that Joe was the kind of guy who would more than try the patience of a saint anyway.

The following day I was taken to see a very wonderful widow, a remarkable woman, I was assured, a scientist. Mrs van Byle Shearing had blue hair and the kind of make-up worn by streetwalkers. She was overweight and sustained herself during our visit with fudge. I wondered what sort of scientist she was. She obviously wasn't a doctor or a nutritionist. She was hung with precious stones. Were they perhaps her perks as a geologist? But she didn't look mobile enough ever to have made a career out of prospecting.

The mystery deepened. Mrs van Byle Shearing's conversation didn't betray any academic background and if she was 'one of the city's most outstanding scientists' as my hostess had told me she seemed to be doing her best to conceal it. She seemed to have a strangely unscientific belief in astrology and at one stage admitted that now and again she visited a truly gifted gipsy palmist.

It wasn't until she launched into a long description of how she had healed a child who had been given up by every leading doctor on the East Coast that I realised that she was not a scientist but a Scientist, a follower of Mary Baker Eddy, the divine metaphysician.

Healing by prayer and faith, by suggestion and the manipulation of human will-power takes many forms, much of it based on the premise that if Jesus Christ made lepers whole and cured the sick and raised the dying without any medical training, then it must be within the bounds of possibility that through Divine assistance such feats can be repeated. There is no evidence that Christ ever failed in any miracle He attempted but there is sadly all too much evidence that those who try to follow in His footsteps frequently come a cropper.

In 1966 Lakshamanasandra Srikanta Rao, a fire-walking, razor-blade-chewing hathayogi, announced that he would reproduce a feat that hadn't been seen for roughly 2,000 years. It's not every day you get the chance to witness someone walking on water, and 5,000 of the curious gathered round a concrete tank in Bombay, some of them paying up to 500 rupees for ringside seats. His white beard waving in the breeze, the Holy

One girded himself in prayer and then, with the certainty that only perfect faith can bring, he stepped confidently upon the waters and sank like a stone.

The yogi had taken the precaution of walking on water which, in the event of a failure of faith, would enable him to wade to safety. He got a ducking but nothing worse. But the efforts of a group of Englishmen who attempted to emulate the apocryphal example of Christ turned from farce into tragedy.

In June 1974 police began investigating the Family Church of Jesus which operated from the front room of a white-washed terrace house in Great Yarmouth. Its prophet, a house-painter who had been converted at a Billy Graham rally, believed that he had the power to enable his disciples to walk on water and conquer fire.

One of the first victims, a 45-year-old Cheshire man, tried to walk across the River Yare in Norfolk and drowned in the attempt. That was in 1973. Undeterred, a second volunteer, in his mid-twenties, tried ineffectually and fatally to walk upon the waters of the North Sea in May 1974.

But it is not the failures of faith that make the headlines, only the successes, and the successes seem to come mainly to people of humble origin. You never hear of a Viscount or a Duchess with the gift of healing. Healing is not given to professional people—there are no healing barristers or university professors. Prelates of the Church never have the gift, nor bankers nor journalists—although some journalists appear to have an infinite capacity for believing in the power of a laid-on hand or a quietly whispered prayer.

In February 1969 the *News of the World* ran a full-page story about the amazing cures worked by Kenneth Hebblethwaite, a Bedford man. 'I can't deny evidence of what I saw', wrote a reporter when he returned from watching the healer at work. Hebblethwaite himself believes that he is divinely inspired: 'To me it is a miracle. I have no explanation for the powers I have been given by God.'

Why God should give His powers of healing so sparingly seems not to be a question which worries the faithful. It might seem to the sceptic a niggardly way for a benevolent Deity to behave, but there are few sceptics among the readers of the popular Sunday papers. The stories are presented dramatically in a style which does not encourage disbelief. Here is how a *News of the World* reporter described a typical Hebblethwaite cure:

A grey-haired elderly woman shuffled along the drive to the big house and rang the bell. She stooped. She held her back. She was obviously in pain. . . . Twenty minutes later I saw her stand upright and then bend easily to touch her toes several times. As she walked away there was a spring in her step.

Such stories usually include dramatic evidence of the way in which one after another the world's leading specialists give up the patient in despair and then some untutored healer effects an instant and miraculous cure. A woman whom Mr Hebblethwaite cured fitted this description perfectly. Sixty-five years old, she had suffered from fibrositis of the spine for fourteen years.

'I have spent hundreds of pounds on medical treatment', she told a reporter. 'I have been to Guernsey and Germany to see specialists. I have had physiotherapy and worn steel corsets, but all to no effect. The pain is unbearable sometimes.' After a few minutes with the remarkable Mr Hebblethwaite she sat up (according to *News of the World* reporters) and cried: 'It's gone, the pain's gone . . . after all these years it's a miracle.'

One of Mr Hebblethwaite's most spectacular cures was effected on a forty-two-year-old car salesman. He had been invalided out of the RAF with a serious neck disorder and a disability pension. There was a laying-on of hands and improvement was almost immediate. Mr Dennis Betts, the victim, had to go back to the RAF for a checkup and there they passed him as completely fit. They also took his pension away, which goes to show that even a silver lining sometimes has a cloud.

Mr Hebblethwaite also made whole a window cleaner, who fell from a building and finished with his right arm three inches shorter than his left. Not only did Mr Hebblethwaite relieve him of his pain, but he was able to restore the diminished arm to its original length, a feat which enabled the window cleaner to take up judo in his spare time.

As I said, most of the people who suddenly find themselves able to work miracles are hardworking artisans or unskilled workers. The gift of healing came in 1969 to a former circus performer and magician called Patrick Ferry. While repairing broken vacuum cleaners in the Glasgow area he discovered that he also had the gift of repairing broken bodies. He is alleged to have cured six-year-old George McDonald of asthma and alleviated the suffering of a multiple sclerosis victim. 'I can't cure everyone I see', he told a paper, 'but if I'm successful in two cases out of ten I'm happy.'

A French plumber, M. Henaux, also received the gift. God has appeared to him twice. The first time, in 1933, He came in the shape of an intense flame and announced bluntly: 'I am God. You have permission to ask for the healing of whoever you like.' The second time, Christ made a personalised appearance in the romantic Pre-Raphaelite image depicted by *fin-de-siècle* religious painters: beard, long hair and flowing draperies.

M. Henaux refuses to be photographed on the grounds that his face will not leave an imprint on a photographic negative. He communicates his healing powers by blowing on his patients, many of whom drive to his cottage in a suburb of Compiègne from as far away as Italy, Spain and Germany. In July 1969 one of the patients, a twenty-five-year-old woman suffering from tuberculosis, died. Her parents had refused to allow her to be seen by doctors and put all their faith, misguidedly as it turned out, in 'the Magus of Compiègne'. The faithful were not deterred.

The power was given some years ago to another man in a humble walk of life, not a plumber this time but a domestic servant. Harry Harrison is a full-time butler and chauffeur to a wealthy peer who allows his retainer to hold clinics in the £80,000 ancestral home on the North Wales coast. 'It's wonderful', Mr Harrison once observed, 'that a man in Lord Boston's position will do such a thing for humanity. I serve two Lords—one in Heaven and the other down here.' The butler has been known to conduct healing sessions in unusual venues. In the village of Sway in Hampshire, for instance, the local magistrates gave permission for the bar of the Forest Heath Hotel to be kept open until midnight while Harry laid on hands. People came from miles around to take advantage not only of the healing but also the extended hours.

Twice a week the halt and the sick limped up the drive to the imposing home of Lord Boston. According to Mr Harrison he was treating 8,000 cases a year ranging from broken limbs to incurable disease: 'I cure many of them', he said, 'and make others feel better. I don't know why I was selected to have such a gift but it makes me feel humble when I'm able to help someone.' Harry just talks to his patients and then touches the affected part. 'I never', he said, 'charge a penny although sometimes rich people leave money.'

The best-known healer in Britain is octogenarian Harry Edwards who believes that Pasteur and Lister co-operate in healing sessions at his Burrows Lea sanctuary near Guildford in Surrey. Many of his patients suffer from back trouble or slipped discs and the aches and pains that old age brings. Edwards places his hands on affected parts, appears sometime to manipulate, at other times to massage. He is keen that his patients should breathe properly and is not above suggesting a cup of hot water in the morning for the costive or a good old nose-blow for a sinus sufferer.

Edwards also practises postal healing. You just send a letter with a suitable donation and prayer is exerted on your behalf. The prolonged postmen's strike in Britain in February 1971 played havoc with that. Edwards, who employs sixty typists to cope with a huge and often tragic flood of correspondence, lost a great deal of business. Undeterred, he announced that his intercessions for chronic cases were continuing despite the absence of postal communication: 'The healing gift', he revealed, 'is the art of attunement to the source of healing. Once we are able to enlist the Spirit doctors for a patient, the healing goes on regardless of the postal strike.'

In publications like *Psychic News* you can find a variety of advertisements for this kind of long-distance treatment through the medium of the stamped addressed envelope. A typical advertisement reads:

WHEN DOCTORS FAIL, ABSENT HEALING BRINGS POSITIVE HELP. Phil Wyndham's Cures Are Well Known. His healing prayers can help your nerves, diabetes, arthritis, bronchitis, asthma, stomach pains, ulcers, piles, eye problems, eczema, psoriasis, growths and unyielding conditions.

The 'art of attunement' as Harry Edwards describes it, was given conspicuously some years ago to a small and precocious child. When she died in 1961 she was only five years old but nearly a thousand men and women turned out to mourn at her graveside. Deformed from birth, Linda Martel suffered from spina bifida and water on the brain. When she was three years old rumour says that she cured her father of severe migraine by placing her right hand on his head.

The child told her parents that she had been visited by a Lady: 'She has a blue dress and she wears a gold chain around her waist. She doesn't smile or laugh. She cries.' Linda began curing relatives and then as the news spread she began working 'miracles'. She was able to practise absent healing by sending a handkerchief to a sufferer. The mere laying-on of hands was enough to dispel tumours, cure pyorrhoea, arthritis, damaged limbs . . . but most of her cures on examination tended to concern cases with emotional or psychological aspects, a not unfamiliar aspect of faith healing.

Ten years after her death Linda's miracle reputation was undimmed and her father was still despatching snips of cloth to those who thought that touching a piece of her garment might work a miracle.

Another child who also revealed unusual gifts at the age of three is Finbarr Nolan. He is the seventh son of a seventh son, a chosen child in the Irish world where supernatural coincidences embellished by mystic numbers are highly regarded.

Finbarr's mother was quick to appreciate the possibilities. She took the boy to see a farm worker across the valley and Finbarr cured him. A *Guardian* reporter, Simon Winchester, who went to Aughnacliffe to investigate this Irish Lourdes found several hundred elderly people besieging the school hall where the seventeen-year-old Finbarr was giving the healing. Finbarr, armed only with a polythene drum of holy water, set to work. Dressed in a see-through shirt and purple corduroys he moved among his followers dabbing them with holy water from a teacup and muttering a liturgical rhythm. All the patients seemed happy: 'I'm a good 75 per cent improved,' grunted a wheelchaired old wife from Roscommon.

Finbarr's £1,500 Audi car with its sign 'The impossible we can do at once. Miracles take a little longer' stirred up some resentment among the deeply Catholic Irish. But the credulous were rolling in from all parts of Ireland, England and America.

In the spring of 1974 Finbarr, aged twenty-one, made his first healing excursion to England. It was estimated that by then he had amassed £500,000 by exercising his unusual gifts. Fred Hift Associates, a public relations firm, revealed that these had first been demonstrated to his mother when she placed a handful of worms in baby Finbarr's hand; if a seventh son of a seventh son holds worms and they shrivel and die then this is proof positive of mystical healing powers—however paradoxical that may sound.

'A worm placed in his hand for ten seconds', said a handout from Fred Hift, 'will die within a few minutes.' As a curtain-raiser to his English tour Finbarr appeared on television and attempted the worm-shrivelling. Not only did the worms continue to wriggle happily throughout the programme but they were very much alive when released next day. As the *Daily Mirror* unsportingly pointed out, although Finbarr didn't get the better of the worms he'd had more luck with the Income Tax men—he'd been able to persuade the Irish Revenue Commissioners to reduce a tax demand from £61,000 to £30,000.

The destruction of worms played an important part in the annunciation of another Irish seventh son of a seventh son. When he was only two weeks old Aiden Gerard Wrynne's mother placed worms in his hand; when they expired she knew that her child was going to be another Finbarr. Young Aiden cured his first patient at the age of three weeks. By 1974, aged six, he had become a cult figure and the sick and infirm were travelling to Garvagh, Co. Leitrim, from all over Britain with toffees and toys to pay for their cures. Ulcers, ringworm, eczema, aches and pains respond to the touch of Aiden's tiny magic hands. 'Doctors couldn't do anything,' one old lady cried, 'so I came to Aiden.'

So effective are the cures of seventh sons like Finbarr and Aiden that it's surprising that anyone bothers with the National Health Service. Take the case of the boy who in 1971, in the heady prose of the *News of the World*, was struck down 'with terrifying fury by a paralysing illness'. According to the paper what happened would set the nation talking. Andrew, a 'tousle-haired, football-loving 11-year-old' was saved by a lady called Mrs Gladden who lived in a house 'with fitted carpets and up-to-the-minute furniture'. The pleasantly plump Mrs Gladden put her hands on the boy and according to him there was 'a great heat and a vibration'. He was cured of what his mother believed to be several brain tumours. From a limp form, 'immobile, almost without hearing, his speech slurred and his eyes crossed in pain', he became overnight almost whole again; all that was left was a slight limp.

Mrs Gladden's most incredible success story concerned Dawn, a six-month-old Alsatian bitch, apparently doomed to doggy paralysis because of a hip disease. When the reporter went along with his photographer he was able to watch 'that same dog prance happily about'. The story of the dog and the boy ended on a sentimental note: 'When I look at Andrew Buchan and see the tears of joy in his mother's eyes, I have to think again. You have the facts—judge for yourself.'

Unfortunately the readers had very few facts. Was the boy as ill as his mother thought? Was he incurable? Was it only a matter of time before he would recover in any case? Which did the most for him—his visit to hospital for his treatment or his visits to Mrs Gladden's suburban healing parlour? Few facts indeed, but little doubt what the *News of the World* thought.

Various attempts have been made to evaluate the claims made on behalf of faith healers, but orthodox doctors are traditionally loth to get mixed up in what many of them regard as mere auto-suggestion and communal hysteria.

However, an inconclusive experiment did take place in 1966 with thirty-eight out-patients at the London Hospital in Whitechapel. They were divided into nineteen pairs and it was arranged that various volunteers would give 'prayer treatment' to one member of each pair. The patients were not told of this controlled experiment. The praying was done by the Friends' Spiritual Healing Fellowship and members of the Guild of Health, an inter-denominational Christian body concerned with Christian healing. Unfortunately the results were inconclusive. One clergyman thought that the patients should have been told they were being prayed for: 'The knowledge that people are caring for you in the presence of God may be very important to a sick person.'

In 1966, on a more emotionally charged level, the *Sunday Citizen* co-operated with *Psychic News* in a series of public demonstrations of the art of spiritualist healing. Can it be proved in public? they asked. The answer was an unequivocal 'YES'. The healer, Gordon Turner, made the deaf to hear and cripples to throw away their crutches. One man given up by hospitals was touched by Mr Turner: 'I felt something like a hard blow,' he said afterwards, 'then I felt vibrations. I thought "this is it". Today I feel marvellous, wonderful. I have hope now.'

The arrival in Britain of an immigrant population from Africa, Asia and the Caribbean has increased the range of unconventional therapy dramatically. A disappointing venture into healing was brought to court at Wolverhampton Quarter Sessions in November 1970 when Chanan Singh, an Indian, was given a six months' suspended sentence for not being as good as his patient thought she had a reasonable right to expect. His father, according to Defence Counsel, had been a respected faith healer and Chanan assumed he had inherited the gift. 'Bring with you', he wrote to a woman patient who had stomach pains, 'one candle, one piece of Danish butter, and one flower.' The Recorder thought that this was a 'monstrous nonsense' when he heard that the woman with the stomach pains was pregnant and gave birth six months later to twins.

Then there was the medium who claimed that she could cure a man's stomach pains and headaches by burning twenty-four candles at £10 a time. In August 1971 she was ordered to pay compensation to her victim and was given a suspended sentence of four months. Although twenty-one candles were burnt,

C

the patient still had headaches and had lost £210 into the bargain.

A Jamaican faith healer, sentenced in the same year to eight years' imprisonment, had not only extracted a total of £670 from his victims but had managed to convince them that either they had insects or snakes in their stomachs or that they were pregnant by evil spirits. He was convicted at Birmingham Assizes of false pretences and rape when it was revealed that one of his patients was anointed with oil and then forced to submit to an invigorating bout of sexual intercourse.

Anointing with oil goes back to Biblical times, but the invention of radio has brought in a more dramatic style of healing. In June 1971 the London *Daily Express* carried the headline 'Black box cure does wonders for earl's son'. It described how 'to the astonishment of doctors' (astonishment in the face of miraculous cures is one of the medical profession's commonest syndromes) Viscount Newport, twenty-three-year-old heir to the Earl of Bradford, was making a complete recovery from severe spinal injuries received in a car smash.

Along with conventional medical treatment, which he received in a New South Wales hospital, he was also the recipient of healing waves wafted from 12,000 miles away by Frank Houghton-Bentley, a septuagenarian scientist who was involved in the pioneering days of radio, radar and television. Mr Houghton-Bentley, a member of the Radionics Association who tunes into patients with the aid of a 'black box', had for some time been healing Lord Bradford's farm animals. The Peer enlisted his aid and almost as soon as he 'tuned in to Lord Newport's wavelength' the recovery was astonishing. 'He was expected to be on his back for nine months,' Lord Bradford told the *Daily Express*, 'instead it was nine weeks. I have no doubt at all that the radionic treatment played a considerable part in his recovery.' And Mr Houghton-Bentley's verdict after Lord Newport had arrived back in London to give a celebratory party at his parents' Eaton Square home: 'We do what we can.'

One of the difficulties which faces any minority group, whether they are trying to heal by faith or by wires, is that very often their activities have comic overtones. Which is probably one of the reasons why Dorothy Commerford, General Secretary of the National Federation of Spiritual Healers, had to write a sharp note to a M. George Louis Pasteur. George, a former gas valve grinder, changed his name from Huggins after a visitation from the noted (though late) French bacteriologist. At the time of America's first manned flight round the moon George was told by an astral guide called Lumme Zen that the men on the moon lived in caves. However, the prestigious NFSH felt that George and Lumme Zen brought discredit on the organisation.

Strangely, a few months later, in the summer of 1971, *Psychic News* was reporting that the famous American authoress Taylor Caldwell was one of 10,000 people who had written to George after reading an article about his activities in the American magazine *Fate*. He had letters from doctors, scientists and clerics: 'Sickness and disease', he said, 'seems to be rampant in the USA.'

My favourite contemporary healer is Gladys I. Spearman-Cook who not only has the power to heal but is also, in the manner of Old Testament prophets, able to visit disease upon the unrighteous. As Principal of the School of Universal Philosophy and Healing, she sent out a Press release in January 1968 concerning an outbreak of 'flu which was laying people low. 'Re: The Flu Epidemic,' it began, 'this is not as mundane as man would believe, but is the Cosmic Ethers being drawn down by Mrs Spearman-Cook, penetrating the Earth's atmosphere and forcing man up on to a higher frequency of existence.'

Mrs Spearman-Cook is thought highly of in many parts of the world. One of her admirers, a Mrs L. Graham of Brisbane in Australia, once confessed in the pages of *Occult Magazine* that whenever she was at a social where she was called upon to join in the National Anthem she sang:

> God save Gladys Spearman-Cook
> Long live Gladys Spearman-Cook
> Long may she reign.

FIVE

I HEAR YOU CALLING ME

A remarkable document published in Britain in 1973 (Jill Kenner, *Goodbye to the Stork*, National Marriage Guidance Council) goes a long way to explain the deep-rooted inability of many grown-ups to adjust to reality. Mrs Kenner, a school counsellor, interviewed more than 1,200 children and nearly 6,000 teenagers in the Liverpool and Birkenhead areas and she found that many of them were under the impression that they had been delivered by stork. Some parents, probably remarking on the lack of storks in the area, gave what they thought might be more rational explanations. 'I was found in a car park,' one child said; 'I came with the laundry,' said another. Still others claimed that they arrived in doctors' bags or had been bought in shops. Mrs Kenner found the lack of knowledge frightening. To be told by an eleven-year-old that she was baked in an oven and that babies who weren't removed soon enough became black babies is indeed frightening.

And yet I remember some strange foundations to my own education. God, we were told, made us, but Father O'Sullivan who took care of these mysteries for us didn't explain how; we had an image of some heavenly baker moulding us out of dough. It was most confusing. We were to hallow His name (hallo?) and try and understand that He wasn't one but three—invisible, ineffable God only wise. By the time I was ten I was hopelessly confused in a foreign world of Paracletes, extreme unction, transubstantiation and novenas. I spent a lot of time working out where the borderline lay between venial and mortal sins (how many venial sins could you balance on the end of a stick of liquorice?) and what sort of temperature they maintained in Purgatory. I'd already realised that as I'd lost Limbo by being baptised and Heaven was out of the question, I'd have to settle for something in between. Purgatory was like Sunday school on a hot summer afternoon but never being let out—still it was better than the fiery pit—although how could they *keep* burning you?

My first intimation that all was not necessarily as I'd been told occurred one December afternoon in a department store. Father Christmas (God in a good mood) was sitting by the escalator on the third floor. As we descended I took one last glance and then looking down saw another Father Christmas on the floor below. Taller, this one and bored-looking. In a flash I realised there was more than one God too. There was the God I was frightened of down in London and another God my relatives were frightened of in the Isle of Skye. He was the God who insisted that my brother and I wore a collar and tie on the Sabbath. A sombre God who cut his hair short back and sides and dressed in blue serge—not a bit like the God down in London with the flowing hair and draperies. This Highland God took offence easily. Throwing stones on the Sabbath was as an abomination unto him; he uttered his commands in Gaelic through stern-faced men behind locked doors. No statues in these churches, no flowers, only white walls and black messages of impending doom.

So I began to realise that, like Father Christmas, God had many faces. Nowhere are there more than in the USA. Many of the religions which use God's name carry fringe benefits with them, such as a promise of healing or financial bonuses. In the first category comes the amazing travelling circus of A. A. Allen Revivals Inc. whose miraculous feats are far more ambitious than anything attempted by the Carpenter of Galilee.

Asa Alonso Allen, founder of the firm, even caused a teenager to receive fillings in his teeth during a prayer meeting. 'Why not let God be YOUR dentist,' asked a subsequent headline in Allen's mass-circulation *Miracle Magazine*.

A typical Allen miracle was described by *Time* magazine in March 1969. A woman alleged to be suffering from third-degree burns is carried in front of an audience of two thousand: 'Heal! Heal! Heal her wounds in the name of Jeee-uh-Zuss.' The woman leaps from her stretcher and at Allen's command goes to a dressing room to check for a miracle. In a trice she is back. 'There is new skin', she annunciates, 'covering where the burns are. It's a miracle!' In small print in *Miracle Magazine*, which reports the cures alleged to have been wrought, there are the words: 'A. A. Allen Revivals Inc. assumes no legal responsibility for the veracity of any such report.'

Allen was converted from Methodism to Pentecostalism while in his twenties and eventually became a minister with the Assemblies of God. He founded his own Miracle Revival Fellowship and created a teetotal, non-smoking town in the Arizona desert called Miracle Valley. From here Allen mails more than 55 million pieces of literature a year and here are prepared radio broadcasts for fifty-eight stations and TV programmes for another forty-three stations. There's a Bible college with 100 students, an airstrip, printing presses and a church to seat 3,000. In Allen's twelve-sided house is a swimming pool sheltered by a simulated stained glass canopy.

A lot of the collateral comes from what Allen calls his $100 pledge. 'You've got', his preachers tell the crowd, 'to vow and pray, vow and pray, vow and pray. You got to promise God and you got to keep the promise. If you want him to lift your pain, to make you whole, to bring you joy, you got to have faith. Faith. And faith is to vow and pray.' In 1968 the faithful all over America and many other parts of the world vowed $2,693,342 to A. A. Allen Revivals Inc.

Another Christian keen on faith and prayer is Brother T. L. Osborn who, assisted by his comely wife Daisy (the Lady Ambassadress of Evangelism), tills the rich fields of Global Soulwinning. Like Asa Allen, Osborn is a self-declared miracle worker. At his world headquarters in Tulsa in return for

monthly sums of money he and his staff pray for the needs of his
Pact of Plenty Partners.

I found out about the Osborn Foundation when a Special
Digest came through the post from Birmingham, England. It was
addressed not to me but to the former occupant of the house, a
Christian gentlewoman of unbounded faith and piety now far
beyond the reach of prayer. The nub of the message seemed to
be that financial prosperity, success and other material boons
would follow as soon as the coupon was clipped and mailed.

> With so little, you reap SO MUCH!
> Be on target for God's ABUNDANCE.
> IT'S ALL WAITING FOR YOU! Too good to be
> true? NO! Just too good to delay
> receiving.

In case you didn't know what you wanted, Brother Osborn
listed twenty-six possible wishes. Some of them were slightly
outside the experience of the late Mrs R. I couldn't imagine her
checking such needs as

NORMAL SEX
DELIVERANCE FROM NARCOTICS
TO SLEEP WITHOUT PILLS
DELIVERANCE FROM ALCOHOL
STRENGTH TO GIVE UP VICE

Neither had she the material approach which the Reverend
Osborn clearly expected to be uppermost in the minds of
potential partners. The top three demands in his checklist were
LARGER INCOME, BETTER HOME, NEWER CAR. I gained the
impression that the God who was going to accede to all these
demands had changed his mind about Mammon since the days
of the Sermon on the Mount.

Like other evangelical organisations, the Osborn Foundation
considers its role to be global and it claims that it is teaching the
world's masses to read 'at the astounding rate of over one million
people per week'. From the warehouse in Tulsa mobile
Evangelism Units are despatched to the remotest parts of the
world. Tons of tracts in more than 100 dialects 'roll from the

presses in a highway of print.' A special Gospel Cargo with the BIG TEN Sermon Tapes and Miracle films is carried aboard these units which (in Osborn's florid prose) are 'a spiritual combine in the world's ripened soul harvests'. Their 'treads run deep along the pioneer trails of front line soulwinning.'

Osborn's claims are often so medically preposterous, as announced in *Faith Digest*, that they enter the higher realms of fantasy. Readers in 1974 were asked to believe that as a result of attending a mass evangelism crusade in Trinidad 'a young Moslem lad, Harold Khan' had his 'malformed leg lengthened 6 inches'. With understandable immodesty Rev. Osborn has compared his healing triumphs with those of Paul at Ephesus; although, as Osborn reluctantly admits, the man from Tulsa works on a bigger scale than the man from Tarsus.

The organisation is very much a family business. Besides the Rev. T. L. Osborn himself who is Chairman of Directors and Daisy (Mrs World Mission) Osborn, Executive Vice-Chairman, there is Productions Manager Sam Osborn who is also Rev. Sam Osborn, On-the-Go Director of the British H.Q. in Birmingham, England, and Pastor Gary Osborn. It was perhaps significant that when Pastor Gary jetted in to Birmingham in the spring of 1974 to 'challenge the NOW generation' the disciple he chose to accompany him was Finance Manager Byrl R. Johnson. Osborn regards himself as a global operator but another outgoing American figure, Morris Cerullo, who runs the Deeper Life Crusade, is particularly interested in Israel.

Rev. Cerullo, who describes himself as a 'little humble Jew-preacher', is of mixed Jewish and Italian stock and his mission in life, apart from healing the faithful, is to 'bring the Jew to the knowledge of the Messiah'. As Rev. Cerullo tends to stay in the best hotels the Conversion cannot be done on the cheap. The tariff is stiff: £50 sponsors 25 Jews, £60 sponsors 30 and £100 sponsors 50. Mr Cerullo crusades all over the world from the Central Hall, Westminster to central India, a flying testament to the power of friendly persuasion.

There is nothing mystical about the operations of Osborn and Cerullo. Both are, as Osborn euphemistically puts it, 'tuned to the wavelength of human need', as others have been before them.

62

Less materialist promises are made by another American organisation, AMORC—the Mystical Order Rosae Crucis, a 'nonsectarian fraternity devoted to the investigation and study of the higher principles of life as found expressed in man and nature'. The brochures claim that Newton, Debussy, Benjamin Franklin, Leibniz, Bacon, Balzac and Descartes were either Rosicrucians or, as they somewhat lamely put it, 'associated with those who were'.

Following their teachings, they say, will make you a master of life. Want to solve a problem by dismissing it; see without eyes by inner perception; journey into another world yet remain in this one; transform your personality, actually become another person? Rosicrucianism will show the way.

The Rosicrucians have Lodges and fraternal Temples throughout the world. In 'beautiful Rosicrucian Park' in California is a research library, science laboratories, a planetarium for astronomical studies, a museum of Egyptian antiquities, an art gallery and a physical science museum.

What original research goes on in the laboratory, what discoveries have been made in the planetarium is not revealed. The buildings themselves are exotic, in what you might call the Hollywood-Cleopatra idiom, for Rosicrucianism, although nourished in California, has its origins on the banks of the Nile.

Only an hour to ninety minutes a week with your AMORC textbooks and you will be able to master hundreds of fascinating subjects. If you feel like it you can erect a personal 'Lodge' at home and having selected any night of the week as Your Lodge Night you can then 'review and contemplate the wonderful disclosures which are included in your lessons'.

They are wonderful indeed, ranging from such mundane matters as *How to Improve Your Daily Affairs* to the higher pleasures of *Creating Life out of Nonliving Matter*. Like Freemasonry, AMORC has its secret passwords and hand grips; as in Masonry you receive 'most inspiring, impressive, symbolic initiations into the various degrees of the Order. These beautiful yet simple ceremonies have a moral which will linger long in your mind as a happy experience.'

Although the long-term benefits of AMORC are spiritual there are various consumer tangibles which can enhance your sense of togetherness with other members of the Order. You can order, for only £5, a Sanctum Set (2 Candlesticks, 1 Hermetic Cross, 1 box Incense, 1 Ritual Apron) and there are Auto Windshields, Master Jesus Photographs and Cycles of Life Reference Coins.

According to testimonials, being a Rosicrucian brings remarkable benefits. Its members claim to be better tempered, younger looking, calmer, more capable of controlling emotional urges, healthier, and more successful at work than the non-initiated. Physicians, authors, workers, mothers, all testify to the efficacy of the Rosicrucian way of life.

A glance at the AMORC booklist reveals the emphasis placed on mystery and the unorthodox: *The Symbolic Prophecy of the Great Pyramid, The Secret Doctrines of Jesus, The Hidden Archive* (strange truths from 1,000 sources), *Spiritual Properties of Food, Lemuria—the Lost Continent of the Pacific* and *Supersight or the Third Eye.*

It is fitting that the Supreme Grand Lodge of AMORC should lie in that fertile orchard of eccentricity, California; fitting too that a movement which began with Paracelsus should include among its latter-day members Ella Wheeler Wilcox, authoress of those immortal words:

> So many gods, so many creeds,
> So many paths that wind and wind
> While just the art of being kind
> Is all the sad world needs.

What the sad bad world needs in the view of many Christians is a spectacular completion to its unhappy history. Only when the Lord makes a personal re-appearance on earth will things come to rights. These rumours of the return of the Lord have been popular for nearly two thousand years, but like Billy Bunter's postal order the advent is permanently delayed. If A.D. 999 is anything to go by, 1999 should see quite a case of mass hysteria. At the turn of the tenth century the faithful and the frightened journeyed to Jerusalem from all parts of Europe to wait a dramatic catastrophe. Every clap of thunder and darkening cloud, every shooting star sent the crowds on their knees in

64

fright but God refused to destroy His Creation. The end of the world was expected again at the time of the great plague which swept Europe between 1345 and 1350. In 1732 a man called Whiston prophesied that Doomsday would be on 13 October, and crowds of the credulous assembled in the fields of Islington and Hampstead to await the destruction of London and the Signal for the Beginning of the End. The year 1761 was another scary one for Londoners and many took to boats on the River Thames. Leeds was besieged with terror in 1806 when a hen laid an egg bearing the legend 'Christ is Coming'.

The average nineteenth-century Christian believed every word in the Bible to be literally true and sacrosanct. It was not only possible but thought wholly admirable that two un-eminent Victorians, Archbishop Ussher and Dr John Lightfoot of Cambridge University, should be able to work out the exact time of the world's creation—9 a.m. on Sunday 23 October, 4004 B.C.

In that climate of intellectual opinion it was small wonder that William Miller, a Massachusetts farmer and Deputy Sheriff, was able to convince between 50,000 and 100,000 of the simple-minded that the Second Coming was just around the corner. After years of Bible study and some mystical calculations about as valid as those of Ussher and Lightfoot he announced that 1843 was to be the year of years. Many things happened in 1843: Dickens wrote *A Christmas Carol*, the Free Church was established in Scotland, the *News of the World* appeared for the first time but the Lord did not.

When 1843 passed without heavenly intervention some of Miller's associates worked out a new date, 22 October 1844. Adventism continues undeterred into our own credulous times. Hardly a year passes without, somewhere in the USA, groups of the faithful taking to the hills to await Divine Intervention— but the Creator tantalisingly refuses to destroy His handiwork, believing no doubt that we are doing the job quietly and efficiently without any need for Him to show us the Way.

It is not only Christians who have been anxious to meet their Redeemer in person and to witness at first hand the dissolution of the world. In 1962 when Indian astrologers interpreted a conjunction of all the planets in Capricorn as a sign of universal demise, half a million pilgrims scurried to have a final dip in the sacred Ganges at Benares. The day of doom came and went, as indeed it had come and gone many times before, with a singular lack of celestial activity.

Adventists take great pleasure in their wrathful God who will either torture the unjust forever in Hell or annihilate them unpleasantly. Not perhaps a very Christian approach to the future. One sect which is going to place God in serious political difficulties if He lives up to their expectations are the Christadelphians who are firm in the belief that He will establish a world-wide theocracy in Palestine with Jerusalem as the capital, a move calculated to annoy the Israelis as much as the Arabs.

Of course the longer God delays his return the more convinced some people are that He is truly on His way. One evangelical magazine ran a series of monthly articles in 1971 describing in intimate detail exactly what was going to happen:

> The earth will again enjoy a period of extreme fertility, like to that before the curse . . . the desert shall blossom as the rose . . . the instincts of animals will be changed. The wolf shall dwell with the lamb. Human life will be prolonged. A child shall die an hundred years. Note that perfection is not yet reached in this matter. There is still death but on a much reduced scale.

When you get into such advanced realms of fantasy, logic plays little part in the vision. With controlled thoughts and harnessed imaginations, the faithful wait: 'The darkness is gathering. The day-star is at hand. We hear from heaven those words "Surely I come quickly" and our ransomed hearts gladly re-echo the response, "Even so, come, Lord Jesus." '

In July 1971, a Convention was held at Keswick in the Lake District with a glittering array of speakers. Part of the message of the convention was outlined by Dr William Culbertson who cited the war in Vietnam, the existence of nuclear bombs, the breakdown in morality, the creation of Israel, the rise of the Common Market and the ascendancy of Russia as evidence that 'the Lord is at the doors'. Based on irrefutable quotations from

66

the Old Testament his message was simple: 'Those of us who look for His return prior to the great tribulation should gird up our minds and give ourselves to the will of God in a special way.'

Such rigid interpretations of the Scriptures can cause whole communities to act in a very special way indeed. In the 1960s the good people of the Calvinist village of Staphorst in the Netherlands tarred and feathered a woman whom they supposed to have been taken in adultery, dragged her through the streets in a cart and almost stoned her to death.

In 1971, because vaccination against polio was considered to be a wickedness, two Staphorst children died. Citing St Matthew ('they that be whole need not a physician') the villagers set their faces against the public health inspectors. It was not until polio assumed epidemic proportions in March that resistance to taking the vaccine began to crumble.

Given imagination it is possible to believe anything. Two recent stories confirm that blind faith, whether Stone Age or twentieth-century, works on an equal level of gullibility. In 1971 it was reported that a witchdoctor in the Solomons claimed to have shouted a tree to death. He used to rise early every morning, take up a stance in front of the tree and utter frightening noises. After a month of this traumatic persecution the tree gave up its arboreal ghost and withered away.

An even more remarkable piece of evidence about plant response was reported in the May 1971 issue of the *Prophetic News and Israel's Watchman* founded by the Rev. M. P. Baxter. It appears that in the laboratory of Temple Buell College in Denver USA a Mrs Dorothy Retallack has been exposing plants to various kinds of music. In less than a month three hours of rock music a day shrivelled young squash plants, flattened philodendron and crumpled corn. Mrs Retallack worked with many different kinds of plants: geranium, radish, petunia, zinnia, marigold and beans.

But from the standpoint of the *Prophetic News* the most gratifying manifestation came when two groups of plants were exposed to two different local radio stations. One group which was made to listen to KIMN, a station specialising in rock, 'refused to bloom, leaned away from the radio, showed very erratic growth and finally died'. The other group were given more wholesome therapy. They were placed in front of a set tuned to KLIR, a station offering church music, Gospel hymns and semi-classical music. The petunias developed beautiful blooms and leaned yearningly towards the radio. The zinnias on their Gospel diet 'grew straight and higher'. 'There is', concluded the *Prophetic News*, 'in Christian song a mysterious power which enables the soul to rise above all circumstances.'

If plants can develop beautiful blooms by listening to Gospel hymns there's no unearthly reason why a religious atmosphere shouldn't preserve flowers indefinitely. Having persevered thus far it will not surprise you to learn that a miracle of this nature was thought to have occurred in 1947 in Cheshire. For a period of three years pilgrims flocked from all over the world to the Roman Catholic church of St Mary at Heaton Norris in Stockport. The miracle was worthy of Lourdes itself. On the head of a statue of the Madonna lay a crown of roses, ordinary roses from the florist down the street, but these roses were different, *their petals never fell*.

The crowds queued for hours, they flung money over the altar rail in happy gratitude. An appeal was launched for enough money to work a replica of the Crown of Roses in gold. But then the parish priest of St Mary's went on an unusually long holiday and died abroad. The mystery of the Madonna of St Mary's was not cleared up until 1970 when a former choirboy who used to sweep up the piles of money round the statue told a Sunday paper: 'The only reason the roses did not drop their petals was because of their being wired.' The florist who made the wreaths admitted that fine wire was threaded through the hearts of the flowers, knotted behind each bloom and concealed by ferns and leaves. The miracle of the rose petals was all too readily acceptable. Anything that cannot be immediately comprehended is further proof to the credulous that there is some mysterious power directing our affairs. Proof that there is eventually some purpose behind the inadequacies and miseries of everyday life.

Miracles, mystery, magic, flourish as happily now as they ever did. Take the bizarre story which was unfolded in July 1968 before Judge Neil McKinnon at the Old Bailey; a story which might more appropriately have been heard before Mr Justice Cocklecarrot. A Jamaican couple who had paid £3,500 to have a ghost laid and be adequately protected from evil spirits thought that such an essential expenditure might be a tax deductible item. The bill was certainly impressive:

	£	s.	d.
To getting rid of two Indian ghosts at the house gates and another in the car	800	0	0
To removing six ghosts from inside the house	746	18	0¼
To providing a special magic ring for Mr X	112	0	0
Fine when Mr X was 'wicked enough to take a ring off in a lavatory and examine it'	959	0	0½
To putting ring back on Mrs X's finger	298	0	0
To one magic necklace for Mrs X	205	0	0
To changing 'personal ghost' in Mr X's car	425	0	0

The Jamaican beautician-witchdoctor who had been attending upon the couple burst into tears when the judge sent her down for two years. But a belief in witchcraft is now beginning to pervade all strata of society; not the voodoo of the Caribbean or Africa but the genuine indigenous article. Witchcraft both black and white was given a fillip with the repeal in 1951 of the Witchcraft Act of 1735.

At the York Diocesan Synod in November 1971 a Hull priest claimed that the supernatural was gaining ascendancy. 'More and more people', he said, 'are dabbling in fortune telling, home séances, witchcraft and black magic.' Although there is no official record it is estimated that there may be as many as 40,000 practising witches in Britain. Their rites range from mild absurdities to wife swapping and orgiastic fornication.

A London priest kept fully employed by the forces of evil is the Rev. Christopher Neil-Smith whose Victorian church in Hampstead is a centre for combating diabolical forces. He has been exorcising witchcraft victims for twenty years now and has never been busier. His weapons are prayer and holy water and as a curse remover he is second to none.

Believing in Satan is no more delusive than believing in elves and gnomes and it is perhaps some measure of the dottiness of modern society that grown men and women feel no embarrassment in announcing themselves as Satanists or witches. Of course their activities are lent a spurious validity by the Church of England which also believes in Satan—for some reason the Devil seems to be more of a Protestant than a Roman Catholic preoccupation.

I'm quite sure that if there were a mention in the New Testament not of fallen angels but of fallen goblins, there would be covens of Goblinists and some vicar would set himself up as an expert goblin vanquisher. Meanwhile we must make do with the Devil in whom there still seems to be a great deal of lunatic mileage left.

The titillating compulsion of many witches to perform their rites in the nude has always fascinated Fleet Street. The sight of a lot of elderly people with sagging bosoms and flabby buttocks tripping round a table in a suburban living room may not be stimulating enough to inspire anything but deep sympathy but it does improve the circulation. When journalists do a witch story they usually pick on a housewife who lives an otherwise eminently respectable life in somewhere like Weston-super-Mare or Dollis Hill. Thus *Life International* chose suburban Mrs Ray Bone as their archetypal British witch. 'One or two narrow types think I'm a nut case,' Mrs Bone told them as she posed with her dog and shopping basket outside her Victorian home in Trinity Road, Tooting, 'but generally I am quite accepted.'

Not quite accepted was an Essex woman whom the *People* featured in August 1971 under the headlines 'Look what teacher's up to SHE'S A WITCH'. A picture showed a Mrs Booth and her husband initiating a longhaired nude youth (his pudenda censored for family reading by a large black rectangle) into their coven. The wife claimed that she had been sacked from her job as an infant teacher because she was a witch. Another picture in the *People* showing her about to whip the bound and naked lad in the drawing room of her Hornchurch house seemed hardly likely to encourage an improvement in her relations with the Havering education authorities. However, she and her crane-driver husband had high hopes for their coven. 'We hope it will grow', Mr Booth told the *People* reporter. Mrs Booth claimed that she turned to witchcraft after being disillusioned by the Church of England and Mormonism.

One of England's leading witches, Gerald Brousseau Gardner, who died in February 1964, pictured the average witch as a conservative sort of citizen:

> The witch wants quiet, regular, ordinary good government with everyone happy, plenty of fun and games, all fear of death being taken away. As you grow older, you rather welcome the idea of death as an abode of peace and rest, where you grow young again, ready to return for another round on earth.

Of late an unholy marriage has arisen between demonology and pornography which wouldn't appeal to quiet ordinary people at all. Not untypical of a magazine which uses the market for things occult as a platform for soft porn is *Witchcraft*, which in a recent issue featured the unusual experiences of a young girl seeking a secretarial post ('I heard the leather hiss through the air and a split-second later it cracked across my bottom'); the adventures of a young maiden who infiltrates a lesbian coven ('Are you crazy? What's wrong with a good man, anyway? I don't think I'm that kinky yet'); the daily jottings of a reporter on a local newspaper ('You were told to cease your senseless ridicule of witchcraft; now we will try other methods. There was a sudden muted swish as the birch descended. . . .'), and various other pegs on which to hang a series of full frontal nudes.

The deepening interest in occidental witchcraft, with or without sexual overtones, is matched by a newfound interest in the Orient and in particular what has become known as the Hare Krishna Movement. Although it draws its inspiration from India and the Founder-Ācārya, His Divine Grace A. C. Bhaktivedanta Swami Prabhupāda, is an Indian, its commercial headquarters are in Brooklyn. Its manifestations in London are small bands of shaven youngsters in grubby yellow robes walking endlessly up and down Oxford Street chanting the Hare Krishna *mantra*: 'harer nāma harer nāma nāma harer nāmaiva kevalam kalau nāsty eva nāsty eva nāsty eva gatir anyathā'.

Those who belong to the Temple of Krishna abjure sex,

money and anything which may be regarded as remotely pleasant. This kind of self-denial has been carried to its ultimate in the worship of a teenage guru called Maharaj Ji who has managed to persuade his followers to give him everything they possess. In 1972, while still only fourteen, the plump god had acquired a £50,000 Divine Residence in London, a Rolls-Royce and the weekly earnings of several thousand British followers.

The Divine Light Mission was founded in India in 1960 by the guru's father. Although his main following of six million is in India it took five jumbo jets to carry the guru's western disciples to Delhi for a three-day celebration. The Mission has 6,000 British members all of whom give up not only their earnings to their podgy young god but sex, meat, alcohol, cigarettes, TV and marriage. The cult flourishes as far north as Inverness and across the waters in Belfast. At the beginning of 1973 plans were afoot to buy a new gold-coloured £15,000 Rolls and a private plane for the lucky youngster.

Put baldly it might seem extraordinary that people could be parted from their money so effortlessly, but put baldly no religion makes sense. The British Mazdaznan Association, who believe in breathing and shaking their way to heaven, and the Society for Proclaiming Britain in Israel, who believe that every Anglo-Saxon is a direct descendant of King David, cannot be shaken in their faith any more than the few remaining members of the Flat Earth Society can be logically convinced that they are not living on a celestial plate.

Great scope for all those with a vested interest in a life beyond the grave was provided in 1966 by the publication of the last will and testament of an eccentric Arizona prospector. Before disappearing on his last trip into the mountains Mr James Kidd left a $200,000 estate to anyone who could initiate research 'for some scientific proof of a soul of a human body leaving it at death'.

Leading the forty-one claimants was the State University's Board of Regents who said they would like to use the windfall to provide a fund for a Chair of Philosophy. They were hotly pursued by a motley band of spiritualists, Christians and charitable foundations of varying degrees of derangement.

72

Loudly pressing its claim was the University of Life Church of Phoenix, Arizona, whose founder Mr Richard Ireland, predicted that it was only a matter of time before they could photograph the soul. Their theory, he said, 'owes much to the work of Dr Bagnall of England, who about 100 years ago developed a bluish purplish dye to cover a plastic solenoid sheet, and through this he was able to see the aura of material objects or physical beings.'

Mrs Nora Higgins, a spiritualist of Branscomb, California, alleged that Mr Kidd had called on a Tuesday in a disembodied state at her home. He only stayed a moment before disappearing in a white fluorescent light through the roof. Another claimant was Mrs Jean Bright who was prepared to bring forward in court a dentist friend eager to perform any experiment to convince the disbelieving. As her friend had passed over the year before she seemed to have the edge over Ludwig Rosecrans, a goldminer from Apache Junction, who proposed to prove the existence of the soul by establishing that the world had gone mad.

.

SIX

SOMETHING FOR NOTHING

There's very little difference between the pensioner bent over her bingo card in a draughty hall and the wealthy gambler placing £1,000 on the turn of a wheel in a Mayfair club. Both share with the rest of the betting classes a childlike optimism that soon their number will come up.

No amount of rational argument that they are more likely to lose than to win can put them off. Racecourses and dogtracks are thronged with punters who have studied form and know a winner when they see one. Casinos have an irresistible attraction for those with a system. In this way an irrational activity is made to appear rational. Sometimes of course it works. I once used to frequent a racetrack where at every meeting there was a jockey's benefit. Theoretically had you become privy to the name of the jockey whom the other jockeys had elected to win the 3.30, you would have been able to make a substantial amount of money. But the jockeys kept such professional secrets to themselves, as indeed they kept all the vital information to themselves.

I spent many a Saturday afternoon working with an eminent racing correspondent whose function was to provide commentaries for radio listeners. My numbing task was to read out a list of the runners and riders while the great man scanned the enclosure and waited for the nags to come under starter's orders. He is gone now, long since called to the finishing post by the Great Trainer, but one memory remains with me. Although he figured in the daily prints under a variety of pseudonyms (Captain Cambridge, Aintree Scout and Stable Choice to name only a few) he never vouchsafed me a single winner.

Peering through his binoculars he would give a little whinny and say, 'Well if ever I saw a horse with his hoofs in the — till it's Pink Gin.' This was almost a ritual guarantee that Pink Gin, far from being placed, would suffer some dramatic catastrophe— like having to be shot after a particularly nasty fall. Once after Captain Cambridge gave me four losers in succession even he began to have doubts: 'Must be fixed,' he kept muttering as horse after horse failed him, 'Must be fixed!'

And yet all over the world racecourse tipsters have a huge and grateful following, despite the fact that you are more likely to lose money by taking professional advice than by sticking a series of blunt pins into the racing pages. This must be the ultimate in faith, that a Captain Barnacle or a Major Paddock should be able to sell you losers season after season and still command your loyalty. Even the dismal analysis of British racing tipsters once published by the Consumers' Association didn't dampen the racing public's ardour. The CA took a thirteen-year period from 1947 to 1959 and examined the 'nap' selection of twenty-three racing correspondents from twenty daily newspapers. 'Nap' is the word used to describe the horse that would make the best bet. Over the thirteen-year period, had you placed a pound on each horse recommended by the tipster of your choice, your losses would have ranged from £26 to £290. Perhaps had you used a pin your losses would have been greater, but most people bet to win, not to lose as little as possible. The CA found the results far from surprising: 'some backers may win money for part of the time but, collectively, they must lose in the long run.' Despite their long-term failure all the correspondents have a devoted following. None more so in his day than Edgar Wallace, king of the thriller writers. At a time when he was losing £100 a day at the races the *Evening Standard* engaged him as a racing tipster. A breathtaking example of the way in which Fleet Street often outstrips its readers in eccentricity.

Apart from fixing a roulette wheel, doping a dog, bribing a postman to antedate a football coupon, marking the cards or in some way loading the dice in your favour, gambling remains subject to luck and the law of averages. This is a fact that an extraordinarily large number of people refuse to accept; their faith in some scheme which is going to make them wealthy overnight is unlimited and matched only by the large numbers of confidence tricksters who are ready to feed their delusions.

Many gambles which at first glance seem foolproof contain a small but fatal flaw. Take the money-spinner evolved by a man known to the Press because of his gold knobbed cane and glittering Rolls-Royce as 'Gentleman Bob'. He called it ASOLOC, Arithmetical Sequence Over-riding Laws Of Chance. Simple enough to be taught to a child of twelve in ten minutes. Gentleman Bob drove round Britain selling his secret at £1,000 a time. A salty talker (he had graduated from the fluent showrooms of the secondhand car trade), Gentleman Bob claimed to have inherited his system from a little old widow lady who was always breaking the bank at Monte Carlo.

He did not confine his activities to England. Danes were also given an opportunity, as an advertisement in the Copenhagen papers said, to enjoy 'a worry-free life on the Riviera or place of your choice'. One of the announcements claimed that the system 'continually and consistently earns—not a fortune—but a steady unlimited income at roulette or *trente et quarante*. It is the Secret Mathematical Sequence that has been banned by casinos in England (but not in Europe)'. Wily English, foolish foreigners!

The question that springs to the mind when someone tries to sell you a foolproof bank-beating system is: 'Well, if it's all that good why aren't you working the tables yourself?' A question which a *Sunday Mirror* investigator put to Gentleman Bob. The answer was devastatingly logical. 'Why should I flog myself to death at the hot and boring casino tables when I can make £2,000 a day tax-free selling my sequence?'

Equally specious promises were made by a bogus Major who ran three Pools Clubs to which the public were invited to contribute. The details came to light in 1968 when the Major and his son were charged with fraudulent conversion and conspiracy to defraud. The thirteen-day trial at Taunton and the seventeen-day re-trial at Bristol cost £50,000.

Thousands of gamblers invested money every week in the hope of picking up extravagantly impossible rewards. Letters sent to prospective clients guaranteed winnings: 'If you fail to share either a first, second or third dividend every week that you enter your money will be returned in full.' One of the promises was a weekly win of between £20 and £40 in return for a weekly £25 investment. To bring the Major to justice 70 million pools coupons were checked and the police collected a dossier weighing half a ton in the three years they worked on the case. Some of the money that flowed in was used to buy a mansion with thirteen acres of land and three staff cottages. In five years one of the Major's companies had received over a quarter of a million pounds in stake money from all over Britain—only a minute portion of which was spent on the pools. When investors wrote to claim their winnings they were fobbed off with offers of even more lucrative investment in other gambling activities. All together over a period of ten years the bogus Major paid £790,000 into his fourteen bank accounts and the assumption is that he netted even more money in cash.

Just as in the old days of flea circuses no self-respecting proprietor would set himself up in business without giving himself an academic title (Prof. Axel's Flea Circus Direct from The Capitals of Europe), so tipsters feel unprotected without an army rank. As we've seen there was the bogus Major (Pools Consultant and Racing Commissioner) and there was 'Colonel R. A. Rawlins', a pseudonym which concealed the identity of two Nottingham men.

'Colonel Rawlins' distributed leaflets which offered advice on how to earn £20,000 a year in return for investing £1. The formula was simple and not terribly criminal: 'Send out your own circulars offering for £1 to give advice on how to earn £20,000 a year. . . .' The two men were brought to book and having pleaded guilty to six charges and asked for 619 other cases to be taken into account were admonished.

Another advertisement which brought in thousands of pounds

in the late 1960s and early 1970s to a syndicate based on the continent ran: 'Invest £3 and earn hundreds.' Brochures were sent all over the country from an accommodation address in the West End of London. They claimed that the scheme was based on a 'fantastically ingenious idea being played by millions of people all over the world'.

It was indeed ingenious. Advertisements appeared in local papers offering part-time employment in which the remuneration would be gratifyingly large. In return for a £3 outlay 729 people would each send you a £1 postal order. The £729 which was supposed to arrive in three or four weeks never turned up, but by then each victim had bought a list of names for £1 and given a further £1 to the syndicate and had usually been persuaded to sell three more lists to other victims.

Around Christmas time in 1970 tens of thousands of people were involved in the scheme and neither the Fraud Squad nor the Director of Public Prosecutions could find anything untoward in it. As one inspector put it: 'Commonsense says it's just not possible for everybody to make money for nothing.' It seemed that the operation was being masterminded from Antwerp and the brochure sent to potential investors claimed that they would be taking part not in a lottery or a game of chance but 'a certainty'. The only certainty was that the organisers were going to make money since everyone who joined paid them a pound for the privilege.

Many of the chain letter schemes purported to be business enterprises and glossed themselves over with a spurious respectability. One appeal for investment which fell through my letter box began:

Dear Business Friend,
    Greetings. Have you ever dreamt of that lucky day that comes once in a lifetime? Well today could be that lucky day *for you*. Because this letter could pay YOU *at least* £3,000. Even if only one person in ten participates you can still collect several hundred pounds. If in doubt contact your solicitor.

This last was a brilliant touch—very few of the people to whom the letter was sent knew a solicitor let alone had one. There then followed details of how the scheme worked, the usual donation of a fee to the originating genius (this one was care of an accommodation address in Norwich), the mailing of thirty copies 'to trusty firms or individuals' and then in about twenty-one days 'IT COULD BE YOUR TURN TO RECEIVE THE SUM OF APPROX. £300 to £3,000'.

The letter claimed that the idea was originated by Rubin Palma, an American businessman 'for the purpose of accumulating capital for business ventures', but, the letter continued 'you don't have to be in business to want to accumulate capital'. The accumulative beauty of the scheme became apparent in the last line: 'Remember the more copies you send out the higher the returns and the more money you can receive.' People were stimulated by natural greed to rope in everyone they knew and the more industrious began inserting advertisements in newsagents' windows to enrol strangers.

Chain letters grew to such proportions that some towns in northern England ran out of £1 postal orders as the foolish rushed to stake a claim in a kind of mania which hadn't been seen since the days of the South Sea Bubble. In 1720 investors were losing their money in outlandish companies floated to extract silver from lead, to make a wheel for perpetual motion, for furnishing merchants with watches, for the transmutation of quicksilver into malleable metal. As a contemporary report said (and it might well describe the chain letter rackets of the 1970s): 'They were set on foot and promoted by crafty knaves, then pursued by multitudes of covetous fools, and at last appeared to be, in effect, what their vulgar appellation denoted them to be—bubbles and mere cheats.'

Eventually the Director of Public Prosecutions intervened and with the help of the police and the Post Office thousands of letters containing money were collected from accommodation addresses in various parts of London and southern England and returned to the innocents who believed that for an investment of 25 pence they would receive £3,000.

An even more discreditable fraud reached its peak in the 1960s. The initial outlay for the organisers was small—just enough to print flyposters, and rent an office with a few girls to answer

79

letters. The posters which were plastered on hoardings and buildings all over the country were simple and attractive:

INVEST £5 A WEEK FOR

A RETURN OF £25

An international gambling syndicate now operating in the principal European cities invites investment in a scheme in which it is practically impossible to lose. Within six weeks you will have recovered the cost of your original investment and will be receiving a handsome weekly return.

The details of the schemes varied but the interest on capital was always staggeringly high. It appeared that a small group of businessmen had discovered a foolproof way of beating casinos all over Europe. All they required was capital to expand their activities. Your money would be used to bet at the tables and in return you would receive prodigious sums.

In its initial stages the Casino Syndicate fraud always worked. Peter was robbed to pay Paul. There were no teams of gamblers breaking the bank at Monte Carlo or Baden Baden or anywhere else. The money, as it began to pour in from all over the country, was banked and from the growing credit the initial investors were paid out. I called at the London office of one of these firms in the first few weeks of its operations. Three typists were busy sending out small cheques and even busier taking big cheques in. The fat man who ran the office showed me several letters from satisfied clients, one of which purported and indeed appeared to come from the Nigerian High Commissioner in London.

Two months later I opened the morning papers and there was the news that the fat one was being sought by the police. At a certain stage in the casino racket the traffic in money becomes one way—the operators stop paying out but continue to accept investments until the anxious 'where is my money' letters turn into personal visits, first to the office and then inevitably to the police. At this stage bags are packed, the account is closed at the bank and when the Fraud Squad arrive the birds have flown.

It is surprising that in these days of sophisticated gambling the simplest trick of all is still being worked. I saw it only the other day in a turning off Threadneedle Street. It was lunchtime and a

crowd of City men were parting with pound notes in the hope that they could Spot The Lady. There are three cards one of which is a Jack. The Queen is never used as this is considered to bring bad luck. The operator shows the cards face upwards, turns them slowly face downwards and equally slowly changes their positions on the top of the suitcase or whatever support is being used—it is always light and easy to carry, highly essential in a game in which the principals must be ready to flee as soon as a policeman approaches.

Apart from the man who works the cards and takes in the money there are usually a couple of feeds planted in the crowd. They spur the gulls on: 'That one on the left, mate, I saw him switch it, go on, put a fiver down quick!' Or if interest begins to wane they bet themselves to show how easy it is to win. The eternal appeal of the three-card trick is that everyone in the crowd *knows* which is the Jack, but mystifyingly it never is.

Far from being on the decline this age-old fraud is booming. One team who appeared at Marlborough Street in the spring of 1973 were described by the magistrate as being among the richest men in London. 'It's a diabolical liberty to suggest that,' one of the gang said, but as up to £50 can be made in a few minutes' play, the maximum fine the courts impose seems to be only £50, and the overheads are non-existent maybe the magistrate is right. Some gangs working the three-card trick in Oxford Street have been fined up to 100 times but there are always new victims waiting to be relieved of their money.

An exotic version of this swindle made its appearance in Britain in the 1960s among the Indo-Pakistani communities in Nottingham, Manchester, Glasgow and London. Unlike the indigenous three-card trick, this fraud was on a grand scale. A Pakistani bus conductor lost savings worth £2,500 and an Inland Revenue officer was tricked out of £29,000.

The success of the operation relied on the joint activities of four men known as the Storyteller, the Contact, the Weeper and the Sheikh. This is how it worked on one occasion out of many in 1966. A Mr Satya Darma had been on holiday in India and when he came back to London he met the Contact who took him along to the Cumberland Hotel. Here he was introduced to the

82

Storyteller, in this instance playing the role of a wealthy industrialist. As they are talking in the Contact's suite an agitated figure bursts into the room. This is the Weeper and he begins pleading abjectly with the Storyteller to forgive him for past inadequacies and allow him to play cards with the Sheikh who is due any moment at the Cumberland. In return the Weeper promises to surrender part of his winnings to the Storyteller. But the Storyteller is adamant, he won't allow the Weeper to play; however, he will allow Mr Darma to play in his place. Mr Darma is slowly persuaded to take part and from the moment that he agrees he is lost.

In the first six games the victim is told not to accept the Sheikh's stakes. When the seventh hand is dealt with the cards fixed in the victim's favour the victim is encouraged to accept the Sheikh's stake. He might win as much as £12,000. The Sheikh then waves a bundle of bogus paper money and announces that he will pay only if the victim can convince him that he has money equal to the amount he has won.

Most of the victims were unable to find such large amounts but they were encouraged to come back to the hotel with whatever they could raise. A further game would then take place in which the victim inevitably lost all the money he had produced. In January 1970 twelve of the men involved in this latter-day Arabian Nights tale were sentenced at the Old Bailey to prison sentences of up to three years.

They had been engaged in an outright confidence trick but in 1967 a member of Parliament had pinpointed the biggest con of all, and one surrounded by a framework of respectability. 'In the City of London', he claimed, 'the Fraud Squad is so busy that unless the fraud complained of is over £1 million you can only rate a sergeant for the investigation.' Allowing for parliamentary rhetoric, his statement revealed a situation which makes the activities of orthodox confidence tricksters look like a small-time cottage industry. Running a bogus company puts you in the big league. The rewards can be astronomic, the risk of detection slight, the penalties sometimes nominal.

The same old tricks are repeated year after year and despite the publicity they receive the credulity of the investing public is undiminished. Two recent impostures involved false mining information. In August 1968 the Canadian authorities applied to the Bow Street magistrates to extradite a share-pusher who had been running a highly sophisticated $100 million fraud. Letters had been sent to investors so nebulous in their claims that you might have thought even a simpleton would have got the wind up. 'Your company', said one letter, 'has sent its exploration party into the fabulously rich goldmining area of Central America. We are maintaining radio control and are encouraged by the prospects.' When suspicions were eventually fanned another report was quickly circulated: 'Your company has sent its teams into the heart of the jungle of Guyana to acquaint itself with the working of diamond mining.'

A comedy reminiscent of the funnier scenes in *The Alchemist* took place a year later in 1970. Jonson thou should'st have been living now. The part of Subtle, the alchemist in this latter-day comedy of cozenage, was played by the chairman of a company that was eventually to go into receivership. Cast for the role of dupe was the head of the investment department of Morgan Grenfell, a powerful and respected firm of London merchant bankers. Three centuries make little change. Now, as in Jonson's words in 1616:

> Our scene is London, 'cause we would make known,
> No country's mirth is better than our own.

The fraud involved a Secret Process to extract metal from ore, a process which police scientists were later to describe as 'a sheer chemical impossibility'. An assayer was found who swore that ore from a mine in California known not as El Dorado but El Sobrante contained thirty ounces per ton of platinum, a content over 200 times higher than the South African platinum mines.

The London banker flew out to the West Coast and was taken into the San Jacinto foothills where he witnessed a confidence trick almost as old as the hills themselves. With the aid of chemicals imported secretly to the site the swindlers convinced him that he had seen a 'grey sludge' transformed into silver and copper. Beneath his feet, he was told, was a 200,000 ton lode rich in platinum and worth more than $7,000 a ton.

Within two days the banker was back in London advising his colleagues to invest £1,000,000 in the company. Fortunately for them they didn't, but other City men were less cautious and when the company went into receivership financiers had been conned out of large sums—one stockbroker was mulcted of £200,000. Reading the interim report issued by the Department of Trade and Industry's inspectors in February 1972 it is difficult to believe that such a palpable swindle took place not in Jacobean times but in the late twentieth century.

A less elaborate way of making money is to acquire goods on credit, sell them and disappear. The game has been played successfully and on a gigantic scale in various parts of Britain, particularly in South Wales and the Liverpool area. In 1970 the police were busy investigating the activities of a group of businessmen they had christened Frauds Incorporated who had been buying up reputable companies with credit-worthy names; companies which dealt in buying and selling easily disposable articles. For months all goes well and then suddenly large quantities of goods are bought on credit. They are sold and the company goes bankrupt. Either a stooge is left to 'carry the can', secure in the knowledge that when his prison sentence is over he will be well looked after, or the men running the company vanish.

A man who worked this particular fraud in Glamorgan bought not a company but a funfair, promising to pay £168,000 for the lease. While the negotiations were going through he collected £10,000 in advance rents from tenants of stalls in the funfair, organised massive credit from over a hundred manufacturing firms and hire purchase companies and ordered, among other items, thousands of pounds' worth of fruit machines, 17,000 watches, fifty refrigerators and large quantities of 'flash'—articles intended for bingo prizes. All this vanished and shortly afterwards the front man disappeared too. The police were mentioning a sum of half a million pounds and working on the theory that a criminal syndicate had masterminded the entire operation.

Another legitimate device is the milking of a perfectly respectable company by buying your way in as a major shareholder. The operation doesn't even require capital. A milkman with the right credentials can always borrow enough money from a bank to gain control of a company. As soon as he is at the helm he can repay the bank from company funds. He then strips the company of all its available assets and leaves it insolvent. It is only after months of investigation that most of these frauds come to light.

An extraordinarily large number of people who have been beguiled into parting with their money are loth to heap further ridicule on themselves by having the affair dragged through the courts. In many cases the victim is himself assisting in an illegal undertaking and he would stand to lose as much as his predator if he were to place himself in the witness box. Take the dilemma of the Wolverhampton man who decided not to keep quiet when he lost £19,600. He had agreed to buy property in Spain from an undischarged bankrupt. At that time if he had applied to the Treasury for permission to send nearly £20,000 out of the country his application would almost certainly have been refused. And if he had been granted permission it would have cost him an additional £5,000 in premiums to convert the sterling into pesetas. At £19,600 the four furnished apartments, a restaurant block and two shops on the Costa Brava were a tempting bargain. The bankrupt fled, the deeds to the property were discovered to be worthless, and to add to the misery of losing his investment the dupe had to pay a fine of £490.

But most people who are swindled are not in the tax-evaders bracket. They have perhaps a small amount of ready money which they would like to double or treble overnight. Getting hold of this money, the few hundred pounds in a deposit account or the bundle of £5 notes in the tea caddy, is the full-time occupation of thousands of semi-skilled villains, most of them able to operate within the letter of the law.

In 1968, Charles Spurr, managing director of the British Agents' Register, estimated that confidence tricksters offering tempting but bogus franchises were mulcting the public of an annual £25 million. The bait is usually attractive and undemanding:

86

Directorships available to
conscientious, hardworking men.
Investment required £1,875.
Duties entail calling on customers.
Salary £60 a week.

All the offers promise high returns for some nominal kind of
activity, like strolling about and keeping an eye on things. 'Sell
a dozen house sites and earn £4,000'; 'Earn £1,500 a year by
working for just a few hours'; 'Earn up to £100 in the warmth
of your own home for a small outlay.'

A typical franchise swindle offers the victim sole selling rights
of a sure-fire product in return for a cash sum. Often the product
doesn't even exist; when it does it may be virtually worthless.
One product that was supposed to sell for up to £4 cost only a
few pence to produce. If an operator can persuade even one
'suitably qualified investor' to part with £250 in return for
golden promises he has made a clear profit of £250. The safety
of the game from the operator's point of view is that any contract
can be so worded that right up to the moment when he disappears
he is legally in the clear. Very often it's only at the end when a
victim visits the accommodation address and finds no one there
that the police become involved.

Particularly vulnerable are middle-aged people desperate to
augment their savings or young couples who take a second
mortgage on their home in the hope of quick profits. One con
which works very successfully involves selling knitting machines
at inflated prices. The machines, which can be bought in a retail
shop for £66, are offered for £85 with the lure of free wool and a
promise to buy all garments made on the machine. 'Earn £15 a
week' is the bait. In one case in the London area in 1967 the
clients were given free lessons but free wool was seldom available
and nothing was ever bought.

With an acute housing shortage in virtually every urban centre
in the western world it has been easy for bogus estate agents and
home finders to flourish. When you are desperate for a roof over
your head you are prepared to try any gamble however
improbable it may sound. One man who for years battened on

D

people desperately in need of a home was sent to jail in 1971. The scheme in which he persuaded people to participate sounded simple. He would find someone a house in the £10,000 to £20,000 range which they would rent furnished. He would then instal a large number of sub-tenants from whom they would receive big rents. As soon as the house was full of tenants he would approach a merchant bank and get them to advance a 100 per cent mortgage so that the house could be bought by the principal tenant on the security of the regular income from the sub-tenants.

A thirty-six-year-old silk-screen printer was a typical victim. He handed over £100 in return for a list of names and telephone numbers of people willing to let their homes. After weeks in which he drew a blank at every number the printer tried to get back his £100 which he had had to borrow at 48 per cent interest. He failed. Another victim, an Irish labourer earning £19 a week was sent to view a house to let at £90 a week. A schoolteacher told the police: 'It was ridiculous. There I was in a pair of Marks & Spencer shoes, trying to rent a house at 200 guineas a week.'

What makes it so easy for people of little conscience or moral responsibility to steal from others is the extraordinary double standard which obtains in western democracy. The majority of people (the lambs) have been taught to turn the other cheek, respect property and practise the virtues of faith, hope, charity, mutual respect and trust. For the others (the wolves) the descent on the fold is made delightfully easy.

The most gigantic financial bubble of the decade was masterminded by an American called Bernie Cornfeld who amassed a personal fortune of $150 million in less than ten years. Before he was arrested in Geneva in May 1973 on charges of systematic fraud he had been riding high on the acquisitive expectations of investors all over the world. He and his associates were managing $2,000 million of other people's money and on the proceeds Cornfeld equipped himself with two castles, an aeroplane and every sybaritic luxury that money could command. Paul Foot, reviewing a recent book about the Cornfeld operation, noted that the extraction of $2,000 million from the international bourgeoisie for the purpose of enriching a handful of skilful operators was not achieved because Cornfeld broke the rules but because the rules themselves are bent in the first place. The only criticism of the book, he said,

> is that it fails to point to the contradictions of an international capitalist community which preaches for ordinary citizens responsibility, thrift, patriotism, law and order, but encourages within its own ranks recklessness, profligacy, the flight of capital, and lawlessness on an almost unimaginable scale.

Fraud is a universal institution. It flourishes in Asia, in Africa and from Nicaragua to the Nile. When money can be made almost anywhere in the world by guile and imagination it is not surprising that extraordinarily large numbers of people have decided not to 'work' in the accepted sense of the word but to use the weaknesses of organised society to enable them to coast comfortably along on the backs of others.

In January 1971 a Scot was jailed for two and a half years for making what the court described as 'a career in fraud'. He amassed £6,500 in a Swiss bank, £1,800 in an Aberdeen bank and £1,250 in Premium Bonds from attending interviews for jobs. Living in a West End bedsitter he would claim travel expenses from Wick, 655 miles away in the north of Scotland. He chose Wick, where he took lodgings and to which he commuted in order to process his mail, because it was the furthest town with an airport from London. Although he attended hundreds of interviews he never accepted any of the jobs he was offered—only the expenses. He told the jury that he went to the interviews because looking for a worthwhile job was a job in itself.

A lifetime job conning insurance companies was perfected by the Carlisle brothers of London. If ever the *Guinness Book of Records* entertains the idea of such an entry, they deserve an award for Consistently Attracting Disaster. Their progress round the world was one long lucrative catastrophe. Mirrors fell on them, towel rails collapsed as they levered themselves out of baths. In ten years of misfortune they faked £50,000 of imaginative claims. They injured themselves entering and leaving lavatories, tripping over carpets, catching their feet in lino at places as various as Kensington Town Hall, St Pancras Hotel, the Imperial Hotel, Torquay, Skyways Hotel at London Airport and in journeys to Washington, New York and Oslo.

The luckless duo kept a filing cabinet in order to avoid the embarrassment of having 'accidents' more than once in the same place. Brother Geoffrey had a troublesome jaw, Roderick had a great facility for dislocating his right shoulder. In fact the only genuine bit of bad luck that struck them was in Tokyo where after one particularly heavy and profitable fall Roderick woke up to find the inscrutable Japanese had pinned his right shoulder irrevocably with two four-inch metal spikes. From then on only his left shoulder tended to get dislocated. In 1968 one of the brothers was sent down for two years and the other had his sentence deferred while doctors deliberated on his state of mind.

Insurance companies are fair game and so, of course, are institutions like the Department of Health and Social Security which hands out money to the needy and greedy. Because the Department acts on the reasonable assumption that the majority of people are honest it is not terribly difficult for dishonest people to acquire money to which they aren't entitled. One Irishman who was getting up to £40 a week in State aid using bogusly obtained medical certificates felt so sorry for those less fortunate that on more than one occasion he redistributed his supplementary benefits to friends and neighbours.

The biggest social security fraud in the world occurred in France when an uneducated, almost illiterate Spanish gypsy over a period of eight years during the 1960s relieved the state of nearly 30 million francs. The fraud began in Corsica where Antonio Jimenez Moreno managed to obtain a fake identity card under the name of Vincento Cortes. He started in a small way by registering six non-existent children plus his own large family. More and more dependants were registered and the prospects were so bright that stout Cortes decided to move to a town which would give him greater scope for invention.

In Marseilles he began manufacturing false stamps in order to forge birth certificates to register even more claimants. The certificates were far from professional: one relating to an imaginary child had him registered at an 'ecole poublike de

Garsson'. The operation grew; false pregnancies were registered for non-existent wives to collect pre-natal allowances. When each family had grown to ten in number the mythical father would 'vanish' thus opening the door to extra benefits for the abandoned mythical wife.

Now and again when French officials came to check that all these claimants physically existed the gypsy caravans resembled the backdrop for a Feydeau farce with the small cast rushing about, making lightning costume changes and generally confusing the issue.

If one of the young members of the gypsy band hadn't stabbed his wife all would have continued to run lucratively. But the police found among Cortes's possessions what he called his 'livre d'or'—a genealogy of 197 non-existent families and 3,000 children. This was in 1968 and Cortes-Moreno returned to Spain, which has no extradition treaty with France, after declining to help the police with their enquiries.

The more implausible the fraud the greater its chances of succeeding. An almost Chaucerian drama was enacted at an all-night garage in Reading in September 1969. A fifty-year-old man pretending to be a deaf mute wrote the attendant a note saying that his mother was in a London hospital and he needed £40 to pay for an operation on her leg. To clinch the story he dissolved into tears, whereupon the attendant gave him £40 out of the till in return for a worthless stolen cheque. Sometimes the actors in these dramas are so unskilled that they wouldn't pass an audition at the local Amateur Dramatic Society.

And yet, however inept your tale, however eccentric your disguise, it will find immediate and sympathetic acceptance. One dull November day a man in his mid-sixties with sagging cheeks and bushy eyebrows called at a farmhouse near Yeovil. Posing as a detective, he was there to examine the premises before stealing £14,000 worth of antique paintings, jewellery and historic documents including letters written by Louis XVI and Marie Antoinette. Although it was 1970 he was disguised improbably in a winged collar and bowler hat and he carried a holly walking stick. He had obviously modelled himself on an illustration from a 1920s Hercule Poirot fiction. To complete the travesty he brought with him an accomplice, a 'police sergeant' clad in the type of uniform that would not have been out of place in an early Bulldog Drummond photoplay.

The ease with which we can all be cozened and cheated is a constant source of anxiety to the police. It was one of the reasons why Scotland Yard refused, in the politest possible manner, to tell me anything about the current activities of confidence tricksters. They didn't believe in giving people ideas, they said, 'things are bad enough as they are!' Persuading people to part with their money under false pretences is an indictable offence but there's nothing illegal in persuading people to part company with simple commonsense, and it would seem there's nothing easier.

SEVEN

FOOLS BY HEAVENLY COMPULSION

A British magazine read by astrologers, clairvoyants, psychometrists and those fascinated by the apparently inexplicable sells some 50,000 copies a month and is probably seen by four or five times that number. Between fifty and sixty per cent of the adult population of countries like Britain, France and Germany consult their birthday predictions in the morning paper.

In 1969 one firm in Long Island sold more than a quarter of a million 'personalised' horoscopes. Spirit séances, table tilting, crystal gazing, soothsaying and all aspects of the occult are growth markets in America. A book about the well-known Washington sybil Jeane Dixon (Ruth Montgomery, *A Gift of Prophecy*, Bantam, 1970) sold 260,000 hardback copies and nearly three million in paperback. Although her 'futurecasts' are either downright wrong (she prophesied that the Russians would be the first to land on the moon, that China would start a Third World War in 1958 and that the Vietnam war would end in 1966) or vague enough to fit almost any future sequence of events, millions of people have complete faith in her powers. One of Jeane Dixon's more recent predictions, in a book published in June 1971, is that a comet will collide with Earth in the 1980s. Although Miss Dixon knows when and where this catastrophe will take place, she is somewhat selfishly keeping the information to herself.

Despite the fact that three-quarters of the clients who visit fortune-tellers are women, there are many men who have an obsessional belief in the ability of certain individuals to peer through the veil of the future. An astonishingly large number of business executives retain their own private clairvoyants; astrologers are widely used to determine favourable dates for takeover bids and mergers and the likely movement of the stock market. At least one businessman asks Chelsea clairvoyant Douglas Johnson to come and sit in on appointment boards. 'On one occasion', Mr Johnson is quoted as saying, 'he appointed someone against my advice who turned out to be an alcoholic.'

Tom Corbett, a London astrologer whose crystal ball is insured at Lloyds for £350, numbers bankers, financiers, barristers, judges, medical men and even clergymen among his satisfied clients. And according to Deziah, a Nottingham-born fortune-teller who now lives in America, Britain leads the world in necromancy. She's probably right: in 1972 the number of books on occultism published in Britain reached the incredible total of 165—more, for instance, than on aeronautics or photography or even astronomy. The occult ascendancy of this country stimulated Exprinter Tours of New York to organise in 1971 a fourteen-day jaunt to London. For around $650 Americans were given a package tour of the psychic scene, a free gift of an astrological chart, a seat at a banquet organised by the Spiritualist Association of Great Britain, entry to séances and the opportunity of meeting 'psychics of stature'.

Even the BBC was allowing one of its disc jockeys to analyse the nation's tea leaves while another gave astrological predictions. A casual visitor might think that we have taken collective leave of our national senses. Occult publications feature advertisements for Individually Created Amulets, Talismans and Oils together with lists of rare herbs and 'Magickal Materials'.

Do you want instant calm? A Baker Street swami offers to open a new chapter in your life: 'Our system of meditation is so powerful that it can transcend a man or woman to the psychic or spiritual plane in two to five minutes and during the same period they may see a radiation of Astral Light!' The unfortunately named Dr Rampa, a Tibetan monk, also teaches meditation and offers as light relief Ho Tai the Laughing Buddha: 3½ inches high, brings Good Luck, handpainted £3. An ancient secret brotherhood of the Andes advertises a condensed *Power Course* to help your Spiritual Advancement.

Mr A. Larno (NO POSTAL WORK UNTIL OCT.) announces that he has 'now moved outside fun fair next concert pav. in Battersea Park'; Mrs Weston of Westcliff-on-Sea invites you to 'remove 2, 3, 4, 5 and 6 cards from a pack, shuffle remainder, select 7 cards from pack and list in order of selection'. For 50p she will not only reveal the future but give you a 'brisk analysis of your handwriting'.

A psychic magazine advertises a Welsh Seer at Shepherd's Bush who numbers TV, Stage and Film Stars among his clientele. Captain Bean (Master Mariner) after '30 years living attuned to the natural forces on the wide oceans and exploration in all the mystic corners of the world' is equipped to answer three of your questions for 50p and SAE. There's a Mr Leslie who offers *Evidence of the Survival of Your Loved One*, and Madam Victoria (a member of an ancient Romany family, patronised by Royalty) who gives daily consultations at the foot of Aquarium Steps, Brighton.

The testimonials reproduced by men like Raymond Seng (Red Indian Seer) and Valaura (Tarot Expert) describe the supreme happiness and good luck a small investment can bring. Valaura, for instance, who offers 'a full 12 page reading with dictation from trance' for £2 or extended spirit messages for £6 demands a lock of your hair as well as a postal order or cheque. Her speedy and practical advice is 'attended to personally in strict privacy' and her testimonials are often hysterically grateful:

> I thank God you have been my friend . . . your letter brought a quick surge of relief . . . your advice helped me to pass my driving test . . . you have given me great upliftment . . . we appreciate your prayers so much.

Raymond Seng, who solves all problems clairvoyantly and gives

D*

auric readings from NW 10, has equally flattering tributes to
dangle before the doubtful:

> You give much value for money . . . you have given me a
> reason for wanting to live . . . God bless you for your wonderful
> gift and the kind way you use it . . . you are no humbug but
> really genuine . . . you are really marvellous . . . you are a
> wonderful man.

Vesta, Madame Zena, Pierre, Nina, Luana, Madame Theresa
and Dr Theodore van der Lyn PhD jostle each other in the
advertising columns amid a bewildering variety of occult
esoterica: pasquini divining wands, psychic trumpets, aura
goggles, crystal balls and Tranquillizer Touch Stones.

Horoscope, which claims to be the world's leading astrological
monthly, is a happy advertising medium for a wide variety of
assorted goods and services, many of which have little to do with
the study of the stars. Jane Scott offers introductions to the
opposite sex 'with sincerity and thoughtfulness' and if your
private relationships aren't turning out satisfactorily you can
always write to Margaret Bruce. For 70p she will send you the
best stuff available for sticking pins in—'real image wax'.

Among the advertisements in *Horoscope* for ancient gemstones
of the occulus and pebble pendants ('carry the wisdom and
protection of the water element'), were the hardcore offers of
instant help. They ranged from a Hungarian gypsy palmist card
reader and a Countess specialising in scientifically drawn
cosmograms to sand diviners, coffee readers, Hermetic Tarot
predictors, even a full-time practitioner of Natural Magick. Fees
are not slight. Mir Bashir BA of Finchley Road charges £22 for
an exhaustive analysis of your life and psychology and Kamakshya
('internationally renowned Palmist and Astrologer of great
magnitude') who claims to have helped statesmen and world
politicians charges only a pound less. His predictions are based
on a handprint and 'if available, latest face photo'.

The readers of such magazines as *Prediction* have tremendous
reservoirs of credulity and they tend to be worried by small
things. They ask questions like: 'Which are luckier, odd or even
numbers?' A recent cry for help which intrigued me ran: 'What

96

is the reason for the shimmering rays of light seen coming from the ends of a person's fingertips?' Curious enough. But what is even more curious is that these queries are treated with po-faced solemnity. My answer to the shimmering ray of light would be to suggest that A.E.P. of Newport went and lay down with a bottle of smelling salts while I rang for the doctor. But for *Prediction* that sort of delusion is all in a day's work:

> The ability to see rays of light or shimmering (similar to the air above a radiator) coming from living tissue is a sign of developing clairvoyance . . . by practising daily you should soon see the colour of the other two auras, the mental and the spiritual, round a person in a softly-lighted room.

In this twilight world of auras and astral emanations, of mediums and seers, there is much that is farcical but also much that is sad. Quite clearly many people who dabble in the occult are in so confused a state that they are in need of psychiatric treatment. There is an insatiable demand for reassurance, for certainty, for some kind of foreknowledge of what lies round the corner.

The prerequisite of prediction is that it should be fairly cheery. Catastrophes can be forecast as long as they are due to occur in far away places. Prognostications of misfortune and disaster for the famous are also very popular. *Old Moore's Almanack*, an annual publication dedicated to the charting of afflictions to come, has a circulation of 1,800,000 and continues to sell steadily despite the fact that it can consistently be seen year after year to be terribly wrong. From the time of Merlin down through Mother Shipton, Robert Nixon (the Cheshire Idiot) and the latter-day almanack-makers—Lilly, Poor Robin, Partridge and Francis Moore—there has never been a dearth of oracles. The more vague they are, the more successful, because the chance of their predictions coming true has been that much greater.

The great success of prophets like Nostradamus and the Brahan Seer lies in the ambiguous nature of their forecasts. But for real equivocation you need look no further than the astrological columns of any woman's magazine. Much of what the stars foretell is either so obvious ('you will need a real sense of humour to face the day') or so double-edged ('someone near you will act to your advantage') or so plain daft ('wear red today for real luck') that you might imagine it was intended only for the simpleminded. But a mixture of fatuity and flattery characterises all these columns. Here for instance is a typical forecast assembled from nine contemporary publications:

Use your own judgment if faced with a major decision at the end of the month (*True Magazine*); good days alternate with dull days (*Hers*); encourage your boyfriend or husband not to let his colleagues impose on his good nature (*McCall's*); do not put your trust in any newcomers who may enter your circle around this time (*Harpers & Queen*); an intriguing month bringing money luck at the right moment and banishing boring hangovers from your life at the right moment too (*She*); you are really rather nice when you are lethargic, it diminishes the aggressive streak in you (*Nova*); what you lack in talent and imagination you make up for in sheer hard work (*Vanity Fair*); if you feel like getting in touch with people you knew years ago you should do so (*Woman*); outdoor sports should give you a glow of wellbeing (*Woman's Journal*).

If questioned, most women who consult their horoscopes would tell you that it was only a bit of fun. But there seems to be a deeper conviction that 'there must be something in it'; there are large numbers of adults for whom astrology has a profound significance.

The presumptuous lunacy on which astrology is based was described by Charles Mackay in his treatise *Extraordinary Popular Delusions and the Madness of Crowds* in 1841:

How flattering to the pride of man to think that the stars in their courses watch over him and typify by their movements and aspects the joys or sorrows that await him! He fondly imagines that eternal worlds were chiefly created to prognosticate his fate. How we should pity the arrogance of the worm that crawls at our feet, if we knew that it also desired to know the secrets of futurity, and imagined that meteors shot athwart the sky to warn it that a tom-tit was hovering near to gobble it up.

Because it is almost impossible to conduct a sensible conversation with people who are in a state of happy but unmistakeable delusion, talking to those who dabble in fortune-telling and spiritualism can take on the qualities of a nightmare.

In 1971 Derek Parker, the editor of *Poetry Review*, whose wife practises as a consultant astrologer, undertook an objective enquiry into astrology. He reached no rigid conclusions but he did have the courage to publish an appendix to his book by Anthony Stevens, a psychiatrist. Stevens claims that astrology, far from being a science, is a delusional system comparable to organised religion. He compared the believer in astrology with a person suffering from paranoid schizophrenia:

> While schizophrenic delusions represent an attempt on the part of the patient to render his circumstances explicable and to create some kind of order out of his own private chaos, astrology, I submit, represents a similar attempt operating at a collective level.

Stevens was critical of astrologers who 'instead of freeing their client from his paranoia reinforce it by dragging him into a shared paranoia, a *folie à deux*, in which both astrologer and client subscribe to the same delusional system'.

Another comparatively recent collective delusion centres round the phenomenon of the flying saucer. The first sighting occurred as recently as 1945 when an American saw 'objects' flying over Washington. Since then these astral space machines have been coming and going in various parts of the world; little men have even been seen alighting from them.

But it now appears from the researches of H. Taylor Buckner of the University of California at Berkeley that people who see saucers fall into a distinctly identifiable group—they are usually old and usually women. They are likely to be widowed or single, poor, uneducated and in bad physical and mental health. As Buckner said: 'I have never seen a male saucerian who could make a successful representation of normalcy.' This has not deterred relatively sane people from believing in saucers or indeed seeing them. In 1962 Gabriel Green, a leading saucerian who announced that he had been told to run for office by a visitor from Alpha Centauri, received 171,000 votes in the California Democratic Primary election.

One wonders how many votes he received from the extraordinarily large number of people whose hobby is trapping messages from the spirit world on their *ouija* boards. The *ouija* board which takes its name from the French and German words for 'yes' is used with a *planchette*—a heart-shaped device on castors believed to be moved by Spirits when the fingers are placed on it. The letters and numbers to which it moves spell out the message.

Although the sale of *ouija* boards is nowhere near as high in Britain as in the USA, their use can have dispiriting results. At an Oxford court in August 1971 two men and a youth claimed that they consulted a *ouija* board on all important matters. It had confirmed their plans to rob a Post Office, a corroboration which turned out to be both wrong and costly. A strange story, but even stranger was the reaction of Mr Gordon Adams, secretary of the company which publishes *Psychic News*. He said that *ouija* boards were unreliable because they used 'a lower form of vibration' which could be manipulated by mischievous spirits. 'There are', he said, 'mischievous people on the other side just as there are on *this* side of life.'

The amount of mischief that can befall those who believe in the existence of a person-to-person message service between this world and the next is frequent and frequently tragic. A typical tale of fraud emerged at York when two men were sentenced to eight and four years respectively for robbing an old lady of a sizeable fortune. In 1967 she had been left £100,000. A devout spiritualist, she was overjoyed when she met the two men in a café. They promised to put her in touch with the world beyond and gulled her with tea leaves and bogus séances until she was completely in their power. When the 'phone began to ring in the middle of the night she thought she was receiving long-distance calls from God. On the other end of the line He instructed her to give her money to the two men she had met in the café. The men would give it to Oxfam, He said, because that was the charity He happened to favour most. She parted with £42,000 before the police moved in.

100

The often desperate and understandable desire of the bereaved to be given convincing proof that their partner has passed on to some kind of existence which makes an eventual reunion possible has led to all kinds of deceit and fraud. Some of the evidence at séances is so tenuous and crude ('Does the letter S have any significance for you . . . ?') that nobody in full possession of their faculties would accept it. But the kind of people who turn to mediums for consolation are very often in an emotionally unbalanced state.

The most famous recent case in British courts was the trial of Helen Duncan. This forty-six-year-old Perthshire woman first came into the headlines in 1931 when she was investigated by a Spiritualist society in London which disbelieved her claims. Far from diminishing her influence the attack led to a spirited defence by the Spiritualists' National Union; her reputation grew and by 1944 when she was brought to trial at the Old Bailey for offences against the Witchcraft Act of 1735 she was in great demand as a materialisation medium all over Britain.

It is a well-attested phenomenon that a newspaper exposure or a court action, far from toppling a mountebank, often strengthens their influence over the deluded. Some years ago a woman rang me and asked if my name was Derek Cooper. When I said it was, she rattled on about an article which had been written in a Sunday paper by a journalist of the same name.

'I thought you ought to know', she said, 'that all those lies you wrote about me, all that rubbish about me taking money under false pretences and not being a palmist at all has done you no good at all. My telephone hasn't stopped ringing since the paper came out and my business has trebled. So next time you want to print lies like that you'd better be more careful.'

And so it was with Mrs Duncan. Despite the evidence of the prosecution that she had defrauded and preyed on the public, the defence was able to produce forty-five witnesses who remained unshaken in their belief that Mrs Duncan was able to materialise the dead. Among them was the noted columnist Hannen Swaffer who told the court that he was a trained observer of psychic phenomena and that on five or six occasions he had seen ectoplasm pouring from the medium's nostrils like a thick rope.

Asked if butter muslin could be mistaken for ectoplasm Swaffer was incredulous: 'Anybody who described this ectoplasm as butter muslin would be a child.'

The trial lasted for eight days and in his summing up the Recorder of London, Sir Gerald Dodson, referred to one of the witnesses who clung to the belief that she had seen her son although he had never been born. 'She firmly believes', said Sir Gerald, 'it was her son and this phenomenon could not be given a face or a head because it was never born; and now we know it was a miscarriage only five months old when you could not even tell whether it was a male or female. And here is this lady telling us she was quite satisfied she had seen her son, grown up now, some 20 years of growth manifested in this child . . . it makes one think one has almost plumbed the depths of credulity.' Mrs Duncan was imprisoned for nine months.

The fraudulent medium has a relatively simple job because the credulous are actively anxious to be conned. In May 1960, for instance, two séances were held in Chesterfield, Indiana. They were conducted by a medium who had mastered the art of full-form materialisations. Ghosts came and went out of the thin air and so impressed Tom O'Neill, publisher of the *Psychic Observer*, that he asked permission to film the phenomena. Infra-red film revealed that the spirits were ordinary people dressed up in luminous habiliments. 'The motion picture results of those proceedings', O'Neill wrote in an editorial in July 1960, 'will go down in history as the greatest recordings of fraud ever in the movement of Spiritualism. . . . The whole sordid mess is one of the bitterest pills I ever had to swallow.'

Psychic News still runs stories which those who are not predisposed to believe in psychic phenomena might find hard to swallow. Under the headline LUMINOUS TRUMPET DARTS ROUND SÉANCE ROOM WHILE I HOLD MEDIUM'S HANDS a correspondent described in September 1971 how in a Cambridge village he had seen a medium's shirt 'dematerialise off his back, only to re-form in a flash of light across the other side of the room on somebody else's lap'. In another sitting the medium, who must be a fairly even-tempered chap, was left wearing only his trousers and pants 'after spirit entities systematically removed his shoes, socks, shirt, tie and vest'. This psychic striptease culminated in a display of levitation when a trumpet shot six feet into the air, circled at breathtaking speed and then began to emit the squeaky voice of nine-year-old Horace, long departed to the astral plane. At one stage, according to the reporter, the medium's features were transfigured into those of his Chinese guide Lu Ching.

And what is one to say of the experiences of Rosemary Brown, a widowed mother living in South London? For her Balham has become not only the Gateway to the South, immortalised by Peter Sellers, but also a Gateway to the Great Composers. Sitting at her piano in Laitwood Road, Mrs Brown is visited by various musicians who use her to transmit to the world their unfinished symphonies and sonatas.

If you've ever heard Mrs Brown playing these posthumous pieces you might feel that promotion to the astral plane has somewhat dimmed the genius of those who come across, but nevertheless Mrs Brown, who had only a minimal musical training as a child, now plays pastiches in the manner of her classical visitors, pastiches which she is firmly convinced come directly from Liszt, Beethoven and Schubert.

Mrs Brown is not the only one to be getting musical echoes from the other side. Mrs Helen Hill of Leigh in Lancashire was approached by a very obscure French song writer called François Petrie who passed over in 1904. Mrs Hill first heard from him in March 1971: 'It was about 8 a.m. one day and he told me to get a pen and write down the words of a song. This was called *Star of Light*.' After that M. Petrie composed a number called *Golden Wings* and a score of other melodies. *Golden Wings* was recorded by singer Mark Walker and a band and Mrs Hill told the *Bolton Evening News* that she *knew* it would make the Top Ten. Alas it never even made the Top Hundred.

It's not only musicians who try to 'come through' from the other side. Ironically just a few weeks before he himself died of a heart attack in August 1971 while out shooting grouse, Colonel Peter Fleming described in the *Sunday Times* how he had been given a 60,000 word novel called *Take Over*, allegedly written by his brother Ian, creator of James Bond.

Evidently a group of writers (a most ill-assorted and unlikely sextet which included, besides the inventor of James Bond, Ruby M. Ayres, Arthur Conan Doyle, Somerset Maugham, Edgar Wallace and H. G. Wells) had decided to set up in business again. They chose the wife of a retired bank official who had also moved to the astral plane to act as their agent. In May 1970 she began sending their posthumous stories to a small house in Hertfordshire.

Here they were copied out in longhand by her daughter, Vera. Mr Fleming thought the novel which Vera showed him was 'implausible and silly; the style is a tasteless pastiche of the original'. But he was intrigued enough to find out more. Vera brought him other material including a novel by Somerset Maugham which began, somewhat uncharacteristically: 'Hope and fear continuously cantered in and out of my uncertain mind as I gazed from the open latticed window upon the scurrying, fluttering, eddying autumn leaves caught and twirled hither and thither by the wind.'

Vera's mother had explained that one of the reasons why these literary spirits wished to transmit samples of their work to earth was to convince mortals that there was a life beyond the grave. Judging by the way in which it had blighted Maugham's prose style there's not much for a writer to look forward to beyond the grave—unless incarnation as a kind of astral Ethel M. Dell is better than complete extinction.

All these accounts of artists sending their poems and novels and symphonies down to earth raise an obvious question. Why should the departed deliberately go out of their way to choose an untutored go-between? Mrs Brown admits that she had no musical gift herself; Vera's mum could hardly be described as a dab at writing. Why didn't Fleming get in touch with his brother, for instance, or C. P. Snow or someone of his own social class and background—why is it only humble folk who are singled out for the confidences of the famous? After Peter Fleming's article had appeared in the *Sunday Times* a psychiatrist wrote from Vienna to explain that 'in certain persons some forms of artistic expression undergo repression in childhood and find devious forms of outlet in later life'. And Eric Dickens Hawkesley reminded the credulous that after his grandfather's death many efforts were made to provide an end to the unfinished *Edwin Drood*. Dickens's son, Sir Henry Dickens, had recorded:

> A woman medium in America went so far as to push a so-called continuation of *Edwin Drood* which was said to have been dictated to her by my father's spirit. I never myself saw this preposterous book but I was told that it was a sad proof of how rapidly the faculties deteriorate after death.

So keen is the current interest in the seemingly inexplicable that in 1973 the BBC presented a series of television programmes called 'Leap in the Dark' which explored the whole field from telepathy to precognition, psychokinesis and clairvoyance. The faculty of being able to perform feats beyond the bounds of ordinary experience is the one which intrigues the average person. Like a conjuring trick it leaves the observer in a state of unsatisfied wonder: how on earth is it done?

This is what the whole of Britain wondered when Uri Geller, a twenty-six-year-old Israeli telepath was seen to start a broken watch and snap a steel fork by stroking it. As these events were shown on BBC television it was only a matter of moments before viewers were ringing in from all over the country claiming that Geller's mysterious para-power had manifested itself physically in their sitting rooms.

Distance seemed to be no object—a viewer in distant Lochmaddy in the Outer Hebrides wrote to the *Stornoway Gazette* to describe how a long-silent clock had responded immediately to the psychokinetic forces radiating from Shepherd's Bush and had begun to tick. Mrs Valerie Ross, a taxi-driver's wife living in Ilford, found her stainless steel forks and spoons still twisting out of shape an hour after the show finished. Mr Edward Rhodes, a printer's proofreader of Camberwell, hopefully held a broken wristwatch in front of his television screen and found it ticking for the first time in five years.

Professor John Taylor of King's College, Cambridge, who appeared on the programme admitted that he was baffled by Uri's demonstration but convinced of his powers. Bryan Silcock, Science Correspondent of the *Sunday Times*, wrote that it was 'utterly impossible to remain sceptical after seeing Uri Geller in action'. Although Silcock missed the TV show he was given a private demonstration at which the Israeli stroked a thick paper-knife until it started to bend; he also bent a thick key without even touching it. Silcock upon witnessing this became convinced of Uri's inexplicable powers and recorded that as an initially highly sceptical science correspondent his mind was 'totally blown'.

A leading London solicitor, after reading the manuscript of this book, wrote:

> I have had occasion to meet Uri Geller and to observe his powers at close quarters. I have come to the conclusion that either I am *exceptionally* gullible, or he is *not* a conjuror. I have a key in my possession which I watched being bent by him with no apparent possibility of trickery.

Despite the fact that Geller admitted that he was once drawn to a field in Israel where the occupants of a flying saucer handed him a Parker pen refill his credibility grew by the hour. Geller claimed that given time he could stop Big Ben; somebody invented a phrase to describe his powers—the Geller Effect. The lunacy spread; scientists discussed the possibility of missiles being knocked out of the sky by mind power and it was made known that shortly before his visit to Britain a team of scientists at the Stanford Research Institute in California—one of America's largest think-tanks—reported that he was able to cause physical changes in laboratory instruments without touching them. Dr John Chilton of Cambridge University's Metallurgy Department was quoted as saying, after examining a bent spoon: 'There is no normal explanation, no trickery.' Ali Bongo, a leading British magician, was less impressed; he dismissed Geller as a skilled illusionist.

The Geller Effect was reproduced successfully by other illusionists but many trained scientists found it impossible to disbelieve what they thought their eyes had seen. For the sceptical it confirmed what they already knew—there's nobody easier to baffle than a well-trained scientist.

A European who has been baffling scientists for years is a

Utrecht clairvoyant called Gerard Croiset. It was Croiset whom the MacKay family called in after the tragic kidnapping of Mrs MacKay from her Wimbledon home in 1970. Croiset claims to have a mysterious sixth sense which has solved crimes not only in Holland but also in Russia and the USA. He has been called 'the greatest deceiver of the age' by a sceptical German critic but Professor Tenhaeff, Director of the Parapsychology Institute at the University of Utrecht, believes in Croiset. His theory is that such clairvoyants or paragnosts retain a lost power of primitive man, the ability to see into the future.

It is Croiset's apparently unique ability to visualise future events which interested BBC producer Bob Saunders. In 1967 he and Brian Branston, then editor of the BBC's Travel and Exploration Unit (a team normally engaged in reporting the curiosities of this world, not the next) decided to make a film about Croiset and they set up a number of apparently foolproof tests. They bought a letter written in 1845 by a naval officer who had fought at Trafalgar, Captain Sir John Franklin. The letter contained no clues to the writer's identity. It read:

My Dear Sir,

   Could you do my sister and myself the kindness of getting us seats at your Church this morning. I am particularly anxious to go there with her and will you say by the bearer at which door we are to enter,

Ever yours most sincerely,
John Franklin.

Armed with this letter, Saunders flew to Holland. 'What we did', Saunders told me recently, 'was to encase it completely in a cardboard cover with only a small number of words showing. Perhaps this was an unnecessary precaution because the writing was yellowed and fairly illegible and in any case Croiset doesn't speak or write English. Anyway in the middle of an interview I produced this letter and showed it to Croiset. He took hold of it, held it, and then it was as if he was seeing or trying to see who had written it.' Croiset said, in Dutch: 'I have an idea it's from a former century . . . from history. Yes. Is it a man who has been on a ship? A sailor . . . a high-ranking officer. He drowned on a

sort of naval ship . . . the ship is sinking and then he disappears
. . . between America and England . . . 1866 or 1869. This man
has been a captain who disappeared with a ship.'

It was a remarkably close guess. Shortly after writing the
letter which had been handed to Croiset, Sir John Franklin
embarked on an Arctic expedition to find a passage round the
north of Canada. His ship foundered with all hands in 1847.
There are only three possible explanations of Croiset's
performance; it was either a trick or a coincidence, or he really
can see into the future and the past.

Certainly in the MacKay case he was not much help. But the
news that he was to be contacted brought a rush of 'phone calls;
the police at Wimbledon received *in a single day* 157 offers of
guidance from British clairvoyants. The police are professionally
anxious to solve every case on their files and were clairvoyants the
slightest help their services would be in constant use. The truth
is that although all of us have the ability to predict from
intelligent observation what may possibly happen—that two
ships on a collision course will collide, for instance, or that a
heavy smoker may contract lung cancer—there are few
clairvoyants who have so far proved to disinterested observers
that they can foresee what others can't. As Detective Chief
Superintendent Norman Leigh, head of Teesside CID, said after
thirty years' police work: 'No clairvoyant's clue has ever led to
anything.'

But *Psychic News* is not deterred. Week after week it runs its
optimistic headlines: 'CLAIRVOYANT CONFOUNDS SCEPTIC; DEFINITE
PROOF ADMITS PRIEST: MEDIUM PROVED RIGHT.' Week after week it
runs its stories of how an 'Astral Visitor Heard Concert in
Beyond', of the triumphs of long-distance healing and spirit
operations, bridging the gap between this life and the next. The
intense desire to believe in reincarnation is only matched by
those clamouring to prove how special experiences have been
vouchsafed to them.

Even electronics is now being enlisted in the age-old struggle
for proof. An exciting new possibility was announced in March
1971 when a Latvian-born psychologist called Konstantin
Raudive published a book called *Breakthrough*. Using a diode, he

had made over 60,000 recordings in a period of six years and had been successful in picking up the voices of the dead—including Churchill, Dostoievsky, Hitler, Tolstoy and Nietzsche. Perhaps it's only a matter of time before an astral orbiting exchange will bring us the luxury of Dial-a-Voice, a person-to-person long-distance call into the Great Beyond.

EIGHT

THE HOLE IN THE TABLE

In 1952 I went for the first time to Borneo. Hot it certainly was, and the jungle is always green, but the story that a fellow journalist filed for his readers was so baroque that I wondered whether he and I had witnessed the same event:

> This afternoon in the Green Hell that is Sarawak a hundred headhunters clad only in revealing beads, the women nude from their slender waists upwards, took Kuching by storm. Never before had they made the three month journey in hollowed-out log canoes from the Lost World that is their impenetrable home on the Bario uplands. Their ears hideously distended and cleft with leopards' teeth, their almost naked bodies tattooed with woad, they appeared bewildered as they met white men for the first time.

All I'd seen was some fairly pleasant Kenyahs who seldom came to Kuching town mainly because they found it a rather dull place and were very well adjusted where they were. As for headhunting, most of them would have run a mile rather than cut off anyone's little finger.

Perhaps I just hadn't got a nose for a good story, perhaps I didn't know a good Green Hell when I saw one. But then I remembered *Scoop* and Evelyn Waugh's Lord Copper: when you work for the *Beast* even the most ordinary events take on an extraordinary quality. All of which sprang to mind when I opened my *News of the World* on the morning of 1 August 1971, right in the middle of the newspaper silly season.

'ADVENTURE!' screamed the front page in headlines large enough to herald the Second Coming, 'WE FIND THE LOST WORLD.' My breath began to bate as I read, along with 6,170,890 other readers, how reporter John Lisners was poised for the most awe-inspiring—and dangerous—assignment of a lifetime.

'What waits', asked another headline, 'on the untrodden plateau where Conan Doyle imagined prehistoric monsters and brutal human sacrifice?' What waited, according to the newspaper, whose imagination is no whit less sharp than Conan Doyle's, was anyone's guess. John Lisners was to parachute into the unknown: into a world of 'deadly Fer-de-Lance snakes, weird jumping spiders and glowing-eyed jaguars'.

The stage was skilfully set with references to Conan ('prince of adventure novelists') Doyle who wrote a 'best-seller that has thrilled millions of hearts in boyhood'. Infested with 'the most poisonous forms of life on earth' this 'Gateway To Hell' was obviously going to be splendid seaside reading for weeks to come. There were even hopeful suggestions that with any luck the reporter might be tossed screaming to his death by savage tribes, which would be sad for him but good for the paper.

It was only six days before the *News of the World* found out what really was waiting. It was Mark Russell-Scarr on page 7 of that other popular campaigning Sunday paper the *People* (circulation 4,946,000). He revealed that far from being a Lost World, the Roraima plateau has been almost infested with visitors since 1884. 'The thing about Roraima', wrote Mr Russell-Scarr, 'is its accessibility. There is an airstrip within 40 miles of its towering cliffs.' He sympathised with readers of the *News of the World*, who were going to be denied stories of savage tribes and monsters from a Lost World, and added unkindly that they could 'turn for consolation to such erudite offerings as "Caravan was his love-nest" and "Naked sprinter gets run in".'

The *People* itself had been given a very bumpy ride some years

before by two Singapore journalists with a heightened sense of
the ludicrous. When Arthur Helliwell, star columnist of the
paper, arrived in the East he was taken out to a Chinese
restaurant where he expressed interest in the small circular hole in
the centre of the table. What his hosts told him sent him
pounding back to his typewriter in Raffles Hotel to file an
indignant dispatch from the heart of what he christened Snob
City. It was March 1952, the height of the Malayan Emergency,
and Helliwell composed a savage indictment of 'The Old School
Tie boors and bores' who were 'wallowing in fantastic luxury,
sipping gin-slings until midnight'.

But it was the opening paragraphs of Helliwell's colourful
piece that outraged Britain. 'In his Arabian Nights palace out at
Queen Astrid Park tonight', wrote Helliwell, 'one of Singapore's
many Chinese multi-millionaires is giving a party to celebrate the
birth of a son. The *pièce de résistance* at the twenty-course
banquet will be—forgive me if I put you off your Sunday
morning bacon and egg—*live monkey's brains*. They are said to
increase virility.'

Helliwell went on to describe how the guests would sit round a
table with a small hole cut in the middle: 'Beneath will squat a
little Chinese boy with a basketful of live monkeys. At intervals he
will push one of them through the hole until the top of his head is
showing. Then the host will slice neatly through the skull with
one swing of a razor-sharp knife—and everyone will dip into
still-warm brains with long silver spoons.'

The documentation was vivid—the razor-sharp knife, the long
silver spoon, the little boy with the basket. One of the two
journalists who regaled Helliwell with this grisly folk-myth
recalled the occasion for me: 'We said they *cracked* the skull, but
I like Arthur's "razor-sharp knife", a good touch that. He
changed our chopsticks to "long silver spoons", slightly warmed
perhaps? What he left out is the only thing that really lends the
whole spurious story any semblance of credibility and that is, of
course, that the Chinese regard the monkey as being the wisest of
creatures. Poor Arthur, it all caused quite a stir.'

The *Straits Times*, the paper for which the two journalists
worked, reprinted the story, the Chinese millionaires in

Singapore rang their lawyers and the *People* was deluged with protests from outraged British animal-lovers. Eventually on 6 April they claimed that they'd found a London journalist who had indeed been to such a party. 'So much', said the *People*, 'for the screams of denial and protest from Singapore. Will Malayan papers please copy!' The name of the anonymous London journalist who had attended this bizarre feast was never given. Which goes to prove I suppose, that you should never trust a journalist. And the hole in the table? Just the right size to take a charcoal brazier for the Chinese equivalent of fondue cooking.

Helliwell's story was of course readily acceptable to a readership reared on Sax Rohmer and the wickedness of Fu Manchu; everyone knew that Chinamen ate puppy dogs, why should they refuse monkey brains? Nineteen years after Helliwell's Singapore story the British press carried an equally preposterous anecdote about a Swiss couple called Hans and Erna W.

They had gone into a Hong Kong restaurant and pointing to their poodle Rosa, made eating gestures. What *they* meant was that the dog was hungry and needed to be fed. The waiter grinned, picked up the dog, bore it away and half an hour later returned with their main course. It was Rosa garnished with bamboo shoots and anointed with soya sauce. The couple left the restaurant and caught the next plane back to Zürich in, as they told the newspaper *Blick*, a state of deep emotional shock.

In England the *Daily Mail* ran the story under the irreverent head: 'The Velly Solly Tale of the Crispy Poodle'. The *Guardian*, more sceptically, ran it as 'A Sweet and Sour Shaggy Dog Story'. Like the monkey business it doesn't bear examination; it exists solely to confirm one's deep-rooted suspicions—the Chinese are heathens who don't know how to behave.

We all have a great yearning to be astonished and titillated, and journalists are as enthusiastic as their readers in the pursuit of the curious. A Ramsgate pet-shop owner who advertised a 'half cat-half dog' was delighted with the reaction. Scores of journalists rushed to Kent; Mr Tutt and his 'puppy cats' were seen by millions on television news.

113

'Here', said the *Daily Sketch*, 'are the animals experts said could never be bred.' Tutt told journalists that the father was a Scots terrier, the mother an ordinary black cat. He pointed out that they had the claws, tail and whiskers of a cat and face and ears of a dog, an achievement which had taken ten years of breeding. So keen was the demand to see the animals that he began charging a one-guinea fee for interviews and pictures. 'When the Press started coming from all over the world, I'm afraid it just snowballed and I had to keep up the pretence.' The animals were really mongrel puppies Mr Tutt had bought for five shillings.

Some hoaxes so catch the popular imagination that they almost appear to be self-generating. A folk rumour that seems to be indestructible is the story about the Lucky Number on the Packet. When I was a child the story was that the makers of Gold Flake cigarettes printed a series of numbers on their packets. If the number ended in 09 and you found it they would give you £5,000. At my school we spent a whole term tearing open empty Gold Flake packets looking for the magic number.

I was surprised to find that thirty years later the basic myth had still survived. In various parts of Britain in 1967, a story was being spread that a retired hospital matron was collecting empty Embassy packets. When she had 40,000 she would be able to exchange them for a motorised wheelchair for a disabled kiddie. In the BMC works at Longbridge, Birmingham, 20,000 workers were diligently collecting empty Embassy packets. What happened to them is not reported.

A twenty-four-year-old housewife began a similar collection in the village of West Horndon, and asked the Brownies, Guides and Women's Institute to help. She collected 2,000 empty packets in a week. 'A friend told me about an invalid who could get a special carriage for 260,000 empty Embassy packets. . . . I'm afraid all the village is now collecting.'

The most persistent folk rumours are those which involve Divine retribution, magical belief and gruesome happenings. A senior lecturer in English at Salford University, Mr A. M. Shearman, has made a study of these stories and he has noted that they are accepted as true through a wide range of social

114

classes and educational backgrounds. Thus the story about the old-age pensioner, sole white survivor in a street of coloured families, who has a parcel of human excreta flung through her letter box is told in nearly every town with an immigrant population. It has even apparently been accepted by Enoch Powell who repeated it word for word to an appreciative audience at a Rotary meeting.

Mr Shearman found that many folk myths still mirror the morality of the Victorian era: sex is wicked (masturbation drives you mad). There are few sexual tales that do not end in some kind of shocking disaster. Take warning from the couple who were copulating against the wall of an old house. A slate hurls itself from the roof and in its terrible descent nicks off the girl's nose and the man's member—and that's what you get in 1974 for breaking the seventh commandment.

Another lost-penis melodrama concerns a baby boy who is a habitual bed wetter. His young sister hears her mother say, 'If you wet yourself again, I'll cut it off!' An hour later screams come from the child's cot and the parents rush in to find that the little girl has carried out her mother's threat. Rushing to get to hospital with his maimed heir the father backs the car frantically down the drive and runs over the little girl who dies in his arms. A horror story more baroque than *East Lynne*.

A similar tale of family disaster was current in the Far East during the Colonial period. A family coming back to Penang are dancing the night away in the middle of the Indian Ocean when their devoted Chinese baby *amah* has a terrible brainstorm and leaps through the porthole with her two little charges in her arms. I heard this story in Singapore as recently as 1960. Some stories are so credible that (like Powell and the unpleasant parcel) they are quoted in learned articles. A well-known contemporary folktale was cited at a conference recently by a sociologist—he believed it to be true and so did his audience. It concerned the teenage girl who takes her mother's contraceptive pills and replaces them with aspirin so that the mother is landed with an unwanted pregnancy.

Other stories are credible because very subtly they anticipate what many people fear will one day happen. Have you heard, for instance, about the Government's contingency plans to build a huge and bizarre hotel at Guildford? It seems that a Cabinet paper exists describing the hotel in great detail. It is extremely comfortable and the food and wine are excellent. Anyone over a certain legally prescribed age can stay in the hotel and everything is free. When you arrive and register the pretty receptionist asks you what time would be convenient? Would Sunday evening around six suit?

For a couple of days you enjoy yourself eating and drinking your fill and then at six on Sunday there's a knock on your door. In comes the resident doctor who wishes you farewell and bestows a lethal injection into your main artery. Government sociologists, the story goes, have found out that more and more people are beginning to accept the idea of euthanasia as a better solution than the miseries of long-term medicated survival.

They have discovered too that many working-class people are worried that they won't have 'a good send-off'. Guildford will specialise in a Good Send-Off, lots of flowers, lovely coffin. According to the political persuasion of the storyteller the Euthanasia Hotel Bill will be brought in shortly by either a Conservative or a Labour government.

The current discussion on drugs has thrown up a whole series of folk rumours of which the most widespread concerns a secret factory in Bristol which is already manufacturing cartons of reefers ready for instant distribution when the Government (Labour or Conservative, depending on who is telling the story) legalises pot. When people aren't telling each other tall stories they seem to spend a great deal of their time putting their fantasies into action.

Bogus police, ambulance and fire calls run into thousands every year. In the Metropolitan area of London alone 200 false alarms are raised by 'phone every day. But the prime international sport for hoaxers, in this age of violence, is aboard aircraft. The nervous, airborne for the first time, or those who fly perhaps only once every few years, are ripe for hoaxes. One such occurred on a charter flight from Gatwick to the Mediterranean. A passenger wrote a message on the back of an overnight bag which read: 'The plane is about to crash. I am trying to make an emergency landing. Do not panic but pass this message on to the people behind you. The pilot.'

Nobody stopped to think that this was an eccentric way for an aircraft captain to communicate with his passengers and nobody stopped to wonder how he'd had time in between wrestling with a doomed plane to get hold of an overnight bag and write the message. Several holiday-makers who had not been in a plane before and expected it to crash anyway believed the message. 'But for the sensible action of the chief hostess', said an airline spokesman, 'panic could easily have broken out.'

It's a story which reminds me of the macabre exploits of an Australian airline pilot who spent much of his time devising new ways in which to petrify his passengers. On one occasion after everyone had strapped themselves in he appeared in the passenger cabin wearing dark glasses. With a white stick he tapped his way up the gangway, slammed the cabin door shut and shortly afterwards the plane roared down the runway.

On another occasion he joined the passengers in a lounge suit and sat reading a magazine. The stewardess secured the door of the plane and the minutes passed. None of the anticipated sounds of engine revving were heard and the passengers grew restive. After five or ten minutes murmuring broke out but it was drowned by the captain himself who threw down his magazine and stood up. 'I don't know about you folk,' he stormed, 'but I've got a business date in Melbourne. I did a bit of flying myself in World War Two—*I'll* take the bastard up!' With that he rushed up the gangway to the flight deck, strapped himself in the captain's seat and took off with his habitual verve.

It would be quite unwise to assume that only the simple-minded or ill-educated can be the victims of rumour—the highly educated and the about-to-be highly educated succumb as joyfully as the rest. In 1968 two students at the University of Kent took to drinking ostentatiously from bottles filled with water. Whenever they were in company they brought out the bottles and had a sip. If questioned they said that a postgraduate chemistry student had told them that an unspecified 'agent' had been introduced in the University water supply. The rumour spread that the additive was potassium bromide and any student who drank the doctored water for a week would be rendered permanently impotent. After a few days of campus anxiety one of the students admitted that he only wanted to find out how easy it was to spread a rumour.

No two people have done more to widen the gullibility gap than Alan and Jeannie Abel. They were the American couple who invented Yetta Bronstein who stood as independent candidate for the American Presidency against Lyndon Johnson and Barry Goldwater. Handouts and tape-recorded messages flowed from Yetta's campaign headquarters and she was always available to give interviews—on the telephone. Her platform included the introduction of National Bingo and putting Jayne Mansfield's face on postage stamps.

The Abels, charmed by the wholesale swallowing of Yetta then invented an advertising agency which specialised in selling space on bald men's heads. But their most sustained and elaborate hoax was launched in May 1959. Abel was driving through Texas one day when he was held up by a herd of cattle on the road. A bull mounted a cow and began to serve her and Abel was interested in the embarrassment caused to some of his fellow motorists by this clumsy coupling.

He wrote a short story about a mythical G. Clifford Prout Jr whose daddy left him $400,000 'to be spent solely for promoting decency and morality through SINA—the Society for Indecency to Naked Animals'. Abel couldn't sell the story so he appointed himself Vice-President of SINA, hired an actor to play Prout and persuaded NBC-TV to interview him on their early morning show.

The campaign to clothe four-legged animals (pants for bulls, trousers for dogs, frillies for cats) met with a passionate response from decent Americans. 'There are naked animals everywhere!' Prout pressured them. 'They are on the streets and sidewalks—a public disgrace to our children—and along the highways, causing accidents as motorists take their eyes off the road to watch nude cows and bulls. These animals are not grazing. They are hanging their heads in shame!'

Abel even lectured at the University of California where he was asked how a Scottie might relieve himself in a comfort

118

station when fully dressed. 'We have found', Abel replied, 'that a Scottie, or any dog with proper training, can remove his garment in four or five seconds with one snap of the jaw. We have garments with special clips.'

Abel set up his national headquarters in the broom closet of an office block and installed a 'phone which gave a recorded message to callers. A month later the line was getting a thousand calls an hour—'more than the White House' as the telephone company angrily complained. The hoax lasted six years before the truth finally dawned on the American public that Prout was an actor and Abel had a sense of humour.

An interesting phenomenon associated with hoaxes is the way in which many people will embroider a story with their own well documented inventions. In September 1967 students at Farnborough Technical College with the help of an apprentice at the Royal Aircraft Establishment deposited six glass-fibre 'flying saucers' filled with pig-swill in various parts of southern England. When the objects were discovered there was a rush of eyewitnesses who had seen them drop from the sky. A Kent housewife claimed that she was awakened by a mysterious noise and saw 'an intermittent red light streak across the sky'. A grocer saw four unidentified objects flying over Rochester in the small hours of the morning.

Exactly the same thing had happened in 1939 when Orson Welles's adaptation of H. G. Wells's *The War of the Worlds* was broadcast by CBS. America heard with growing alarm how a mysterious meteorite had fallen at Grovers Hill in New Jersey and how the State Police were coping with the invading Martians. The broadcast itself generated a wave of rumour and hysteria which culminated in suits for damages, injuries and distress totalling three quarters of a million dollars.

Since Welles's discovery of the credulity of the listening public various hoaxes have been perpetrated on both radio and television. It has now become a tradition in the BBC that on or about 1 April the public shall have its leg gently pulled. There was the occasion when readings were given from the poems of one Loof Lirpa. The *Radio Times* carried a photograph of Rabindranath Tagore, safe in the conviction that the majority of their readers would

assume that anyone so eccentrically hirsute would be bound to be called Loof Lirpa.

There was *Panorama*'s famous television report on the gathering of the Italian spaghetti harvest; there was the 'smellovision' broadcast by a Sydney commercial television station which showed onions being chopped up with the object of transmitting their smell through an intensifying machine 'on a special wave length'. Predictably, the switchboard was jammed

as viewers rang to claim that a smell of onions had emanated from their sets.

Sometimes these japes misfire in a sinister way. In June 1969 the BBC television programme *Line Up* invented a character called the Great Pismo and hired an actor to make some 'historic film clips' to illustrate his career. But there was some unexpected playback. One viewer wrote to say 'my aunt was a fan of the Great Pismo—she saw him at a show in Hastings.' Another viewer went one better and sent in a photograph of the Great Pismo's father.

Similarly when Kingsley Amis was allowed by the BBC to perpetrate a leg-pull on the intellectual Radio 3 network he was taken aback by the gullible response of highly intelligent professional men and women. Amis had written a novel called *The Green Man* about an innkeeper who encounters and destroys a supernatural monster. The hoax described how he and his wife motoring home from a visit to relatives stopped for dinner at an inn which had an unusually high number of correspondences with the fictional inn. The landlord's surname and the barman's Christian name were the same as the characters in the book. There were other resemblances too, culminating in the appearance of the fictional monster in the real inn.

As Amis recalled in a talk in December 1973 also broadcast on Radio 3: 'I tremble to think of what might have happened if I'd tried harder to make people believe my tale, because so many believed it as it was.' A television producer rang wanting to know where the pub was so that he might take a film crew there to illustrate a new series on the supernatural. Letters came from strangers discussing the story as if it had actually happened. The Religious Experience Research Unit at Manchester College, Oxford begged for further details and added that nobody had come across 'such a striking and remarkable nexus of events as you describe'.

Pondering on the gullibility of his audience Amis came to the conclusion that not only were people finding constant difficulty in distinguishing between fact and fiction but had already begun 'to move into a state in which they neither really believe . . . nor do they quite disbelieve'. If that were the case and if the stability of society depended on a capacity to distinguish between fact and fiction, then, said Amis, it's 'a rather frightening prospect: reason seems to be tottering on her throne'.

The most financially useful hoax yet perpetrated occurred on Finnish TV in 1966. It was announced that a new electronic device would black out all unlicensed sets. Every set in Finland was then peremptorily blacked out and long queues formed the following morning to buy licences.

Of course, to take in simple-minded people is comparatively easy. The real test of a hoax lies in the intellectual calibre of the victim. One of the wittiest and most successful literary hoaxes of recent years centred round an Australian poet called Ern Malley. Ern died in Melbourne in 1943, unknown and unsung. But within a few months he had been hailed as 'one of the most outstanding poets' Australia had ever produced. The words belong to Max Harris, who published the poet's entire works in a special edition of his literary magazine *Angry Penguins*. Harris announced that Ern was a giant among contemporary poets, 'a poet of tremendous power, working through a disciplined and restrained kind of statement into the deepest wells of human experience'.

So impressed were Max Harris and his fellow editor John Reed when they first received the poems that they lost no time in passing them round among the literati of Australia, most of whom thought them both remarkable and moving. This literary time-bomb was assembled one afternoon by two Sydney poets, James McAuley and Harold Stewart. Both of them held *Angry Penguins* and the verse it published in contempt. Humourless nonsense, they called it, and so they invented Ern Malley and his works to find out whether the Australian literati could distinguish genuine nonsense from 'consciously and deliberately concocted nonsense'.

By the end of a busy afternoon, lifting lines out of books, joining jumbled phrases together, relishing the obscure and convoluted, they had cobbled together sixteen 'poems'. The first three lines of a poem they called 'Culture as Exhibit' were copied more or less straight from an American report on the drainage of mosquito breeding grounds:

> 'Swamps, marshes, borrow-pits and other
> Areas of stagnant water serve
> As breeding grounds . . .' Now
> Have I found you my Anopheles!
> (There is a meaning for the circumspect).

Two of the poems were posted to the editor of *Angry Penguins* with a covering letter from Ern's sister Ethel. Ethel had found the letters among her brother's possessions and someone had told her they might be of value. Max Harris read and re-read them and became convinced that here was 'a poet with a cool, strong, sinuous feeling for language'. He took the bait and wrote excitedly to non-existent Miss Malley. By return she, with the delighted assistance of McAuley and Stewart, told all. Ern, she said, left school at fourteen, worked as a motor mechanic in Sydney and then went to Melbourne to peddle insurance policies for the National Mutual Life Assurance Company.

And so in a whirl of excitement Ern's appalling poems were published, and quick as a flash McAuley and Stewart struck. They made a joint statement to the press and revealed all. Sydney University Students awarded them a doctorate in Oxometry—the emblem of the Oxometrical Society is a bull.

McAuley and Stewart were the latest in a long and distinguished line of literary hoaxers—some who forged for money and others, like themselves, who did it to prove a point. There was Thomas Chatterton, who with a series of olde worlde manuscripts deceived the City of Bristol and Horace Walpole. There was an equally young William Henry Ireland who sold a 'Shakespeare' play to Sheridan for £300 and a share of the box office and James Macpherson, the Celtic Homer, whose works, attributed to a third-century Gaelic poet called Ossian, had a profound influence on European literature.

Many forgers have been improvers who acted with the most perfect good faith and more out of zeal than villainy. Perhaps Macpherson himself is the best example. As John Stuart Blackie so kindly observed of him:

He found the long-neglected Celtic Muse of the Highlands in a very forlorn, defaced, ragged and unsavoury condition; and he thought it was only his duty, before presenting her to a critical modern public to wash her well and scrub her stoutly and dress her trimly in fresh habiliments, of which himself was proud to be the milliner.

And how did this entry find its way in 1960 into the pages of the fourth edition of the *Authors' and Writers' Who's Who*—an authoritative work of reference compiled by the same people who publish *Burke's Peerage*. Was someone fed-up with not making it?

TISSINGTON-HENRICHT-BROWN, Septimus Cadwallader, B.A. b: Torrington, Devon, 1913. e. Privately. m: Maria Grace Stingleholsch. s: 4. d: 5. Adv. in Double-Speak to Min. of Educ. 1939–45; Chairm. Cent. Conf. of B.B.B. Soc. 1946; Lit. Adv. to Billingsgate Inst. 1947–49. publ.: Dawn Patrol; Corridor Trek; On Safari with Jock; Through Ethiopia with Pan and Pen; Stalemate at Sanderstead. ctr.: Chambers Journ., etc. c: Y.M.C.A., N.Y. & Lond. a: 149 Tobermory Rd., N.1.

The number of masterpieces which are rejected out of hand by publishers is naturally upsetting to those who write them, even more upsetting when they see other people's rubbish being printed and praised to the skies by critics and scholars. In 1968 the German satirical magazine *Pardon* decided to have a go at publishers and academics. They posted a manuscript with a covering letter to forty-six of the best known literati in Germany. The manuscript was turned down by all the publishers. *Pardon* then revealed that the rejected manuscript was an extract from *Der Mann ohne Eigenschaften*, by Robert Musil, a piece of writing which the majority of critics regard as one of the most outstanding of the century. Game, set and match to *Pardon*.

The injustices that face a creative artist have led to all manner of retaliation. The most ambitiously successful hoax-fraud in the field of art was perpetrated by the Dutchman Hans van Meegeren who began in 1937 to paint in the manner of Vermeer. Others had done it before. Michelangelo passed off some of his sculptures as antiques to get a better deal. In the nineteenth century Giovanni Bastianini of Florence produced a series of 'Renaissance' pieces which commanded high prices. There was nothing novel in the fact that an artist's works often command a higher price after his death than during his life.

Van Meegeren made millions of dollars from his 'Vermeers' and of course gave a great deal of pleasure. As the *Burlington Magazine* commented when Meegeren's *Christ and the Disciple at Emmaus* appeared on the market: 'It is a wonderful moment in the life of a critic when he finds himself suddenly confronted with a hitherto unknown painting by a great master, untouched, on the original canvas and without any restoration, just as it left the painter's studio.' The painting was bought by the Boymans Museum in Rotterdam for 540,000 Dutch guilders.

Art critics all over Europe and America enthused, and van Meegeren slowly began to release more of his Vermeers on the market. During the Nazi occupation Hermann Goering paid 1,650,000 guilders for what he thought was Vermeer's *Christ and the Adulteress*. It was this sale to the war criminal that eventually landed van Meegeren in jail, where after a fortnight of hardship he made a complete confession. Originally, he said, he had painted one picture in the style of Vermeer, so that when it had been lauded by the critics he could expose the hoax and obtain some redress for the way in which his own work had been neglected.

Van Meegeren proved to himself that the most eminent authorities in the world could be wrong. Since then hardly a year has passed without some new evidence coming to light that there are very few art experts who can tell their Arcimboldo from their El Greco. An elaborate example of the hoax which is concocted to prove the gullibility of experts took place in Brunswick, West Germany in 1968. A local artist, Hans Nowak, and his friend Hans Giesel bought an oil painting of two nudes in the flea market in Paris. Back in Brunswick Nowak cleaned the canvas, painted a riverscape with a bridge in the style of Monet, signed it 'Claude Monet 1877' and overpainted it with a copy of the two nudes which were originally on the canvas. After ageing the painting in front of the fire for a fortnight they took it along to the local museum and asked if it could be cleaned. The experts very quickly discovered 'an unknown Monet' which they valued at £100,000. The hoaxers having proved their point revealed the fraud.

To write like Shakespeare, to paint like Vermeer or Monet reveals talent, but does it reveal creative originality? Perhaps not. But that doesn't stop a craftsman from trying to prove himself. There was the fourth generation Sheffield silversmith who desperately wanted to prove that he was as fine an artist as his

126

great grandfather. He not only reproduced the kind of silver his Georgian forebears used to make, he even authenticated it with old dies. But the deception landed him in court. 'I made all these things', he told the judge, 'as a test of skill in my own spare time—as a challenge.' The forgeries (one of which, a teapot, had been sold for £350) were so beautiful that Mr Justice Caulfield refused to have them destroyed. After he had sentenced the unfortunate smith to three years in jail he told the Director of Public Prosecutions' representative: 'You will have to speak for a very long time to persuade me to destroy that beautiful teapot.'

Perhaps the age of faking is beginning to draw to a close. Although it has been possible to X-ray paintings for some time the only way to really test the authenticity of a Wei horse, for instance, would have been to break it in half and see if it was Wei all the way through. But in 1955 a Research Laboratory for Archaeology and the History of Art was set up at Oxford, and the techniques that have been developed there have cost the art fakers (and many dealers) vast sums of money. In 1971, despite pressure brought upon them, the Laboratory publicly denounced the provenance and value of twenty-five 'genuine' Etruscan tomb paintings.

For ten years an Italian workshop had been faking these tomb paintings which were then smuggled across the border into Switzerland where they quickly found purchasers. Some of the world's most experienced art dealers were taken in by the forgeries, but Oxford's technique of thermoluminescent dating revealed that something like £250,000 worth of these terracotta panels were of recent origin.

They were also able to establish that forty-eight out of sixty-six pieces of Hacilar pottery which they examined were also newly made. A Turkish peasant had been making the pottery and claiming that it came from a prehistoric site near his home in Anatolia. The tests caused consternation in museums such as the Metropolitan in New York, the Louvre and the Ankara Museum. The Ashmolean in July 1971 withdrew three painted Hacilar bowls bought from Sotheby's in 1963 and the British Museum quietly took off display three Hacilar objects which they had bought from a London dealer.

If there is discontent and deception in the world of art there seems to be even more opportunity in the concert hall. Fritz Kreisler, faced with the most eminent music critics in the world, passed off his own compositions as unknown fragments from the quills of Vivaldi, Couperin, Francoeur, Porpora and Padre Martini. His forgeries were thrust upon him by the dearth of music suitable for a solo violinist. He wrote a few appropriate pieces for himself, gave them revered origins and when questioned described how he had found them in libraries and monasteries in Rome, Florence, Venice and Paris—dusty manuscripts which he had copied and then edited.

The critics called them 'little masterpieces' and one critic went so far as to suggest that Kreisler wasn't good enough to play them: 'We heard Fritz Kreisler again last night,' a German critic wrote. 'He played beautifully, but naturally his temperament lacks the strength and maturity to reach the heights of the Pugnani music.' On another occasion Kreisler composed some pieces for a recital he was to give in Vienna: on the programme they appeared as 'Posthumous Waltzes by Joseph Lanner'. The following day Leopold Schmidt, music critic of the *Berliner Tageblatt* accused Kreisler of arrogance. He thought the Lanner waltzes were worthy of Schubert and that Kreisler's own salon piece, Caprice Viennois, was too mundane to be bracketed with them.

Recently a young Swiss pianist, Jean-Jacques Hauser, unsung by his fellow countrymen, decided to expose the snobbery of Zürich's music critics and concert audiences, who although prepared to give a standing ovation to foreign artists refused it to him. Hauser glued a false moustache to his upper lip and billed himself as Anton Sergeievitch Tartarov. Before a packed house he played music alleged to be by Beethoven, Prokofiev and Liszt. He was cheered and there were cries of 'bravo' and 'encore'. For an encore Tartarov whipped off his moustache, and announced that not only was he a humble homegrown Swiss but that all the pieces he had played had been composed by himself. To give Zürich its due the audience saved its face by applauding even more wildly than before.

A hoax with an equally messianic motive was produced by the

BBC Third Programme in June 1961. They announced a performance of Piotr Zak's 'Mobile for Tape and Percussion'. Zak, a programme note in the *Radio Times* explained, was born in Poland in 1939 but was now resident in Germany. He had recently come under the influence of Stockhausen and John Cage and his 'Mobile' had been inspired by the work of the American sculptor John Calder. A group of soloists had been specially invited to Britain by the BBC to give this twelve-minute work its first performance in this country.

To the casual listener 'Mobile' sounded rather as if a couple of people had gone into a studio, made a few noises, put it on echo and left. And that is exactly what had happened. The irrepressible Hans Keller of the BBC's music department had not perpetrated a hoax but posed a problem. The broadcast was followed by a heated discussion, in which Keller revealed that his sole purpose had been to find out to what extent this kind of music-making would be taken seriously. Most listeners thought it was rubbish, but some found it stimulating, fresh, influential and original. As one man at a slight loss for words put it: 'I had a brief encounter with the thinginess of music.' Several musicians claimed they found it exciting, and possessed of considerable significance, and this no doubt left Keller more perplexed than ever.

But the concert to end all bogus concerts took place in London towards the end of the 1960s when a Hungarian antique dealer, Gabor Cossa, gave a recital of visual music at the Wigmore Hall. He appeared as Tomas Blod—Master of the Silent Piano. Among the works he played (on a silent keyboard) were 'Transmogrifications for Non-Sounding Piano', 'Partita in Silences' with the assistance of mute oboe and silent double bass, 'Four Pauses' and 'Six Studies in Non-Volume'.

At the end of the evening Mr Blod handed out long-playing silent gramophone records labelled 'Rests' performed by the Macclesfield Chorus of Mutes—on the reverse side was an aria from 'The Dumb Wife'. I'm sure there must have been many who were impressed with the nothingness of it all.

NINE

IT REMEMBERED ME OF AN OLD HORSE

The desire to change one's lot is universal. We all harbour private delusions of grandeur but only a few of us have the courage or misfortune to act them out. Mental hospitals are full of people whose personality disorders have gone beyond even the generous bounds which society permits. Outside asylum walls, however, thousands of men and women are left in comparative freedom to play out their fantasies. Sometimes they come unstuck—the multi-bigamist is unmasked, the armchair explorer rumbled, the bogus Major sent down at the local Assizes.

Because it is so easy to impose on other people's good nature and credulity even the most innocent joker finds that the trick of gaining people's confidence has a fatality about it; there is a logical progression from amateur hoaxer to professional confidence trickster. But there are still an extraordinarily large number of impersonations which are designed not to bring profit but only self-esteem.

Take the case of Joseph Papp, a Hungarian-born Canadian. For six years he devoted every spare second of his time to building an 'atomic' submarine. When the submarine didn't work Papp was undaunted. He secretly bought himself an airline ticket, told his friends he was going to sail to Europe in the submarine, and disappeared to catch a 'plane for Amsterdam. From there he went by train to Brest, jumped into the harbour, swam ashore and claimed that he'd crossed the Atlantic in twelve hours in the submarine which had sunk just outside the harbour. Unfortunately the police went through his pockets and found his railway ticket from Paris to Brest. But, as they say in school reports, full marks for trying.

There was the butcher and piemaker who, no doubt feeling that butchering and piemaking was too plebeian a role, donned a new persona. He became a Brigadier (DSO, MC and bar) recently retired from Rhodesia and in 1966 made a great hit with the townspeople of Chester where he took up residence. The Conservatives offered him a safe seat in the forthcoming municipal elections, he was invited to cocktail parties and according to a councillor 'women went weak at the knees when he attended their functions'. However, a sharp-eyed officer noted that his medals were arrayed in the wrong order and the Special Investigation Branch of the Army unmasked the bogus brigadier, who had previously been in prison for bigamy and other frauds.

The confidence trickster if he gives a creditable performance can often bring a great deal of pleasure into other people's lives. For a moment they are lifted out of their daily drabness into the champagne world inhabited by the extravagant character who takes them by storm. How happy Mrs Joyce Butcher was, for instance, when while on holiday in 1969 in Hunstanton, she and her husband met the film star Kim Novak.

Like royalty Kim never carried cash and she could never remember to get to the bank in time. The Butchers were only too pleased to tide her over, especially when she told them she was having £40,000 transferred from a Swiss bank. They gave her money and invited her to come and stay with them in their council house in Braintree. Together the three went looking at £20,000 houses for Kim to buy and they were thrilled when she promised them jobs at £100 a week as soon as she got herself settled.

But it wasn't Kim Novak at all—just a Yorkshire-born GI bride who had been deported back to her native land for passing dud cheques in the States. When 'Kim' was given six months Mrs Butcher forgave her all: 'She conned us all right, but I'm not bitter. She gave me the most marvellous holiday of my life.'

When it comes to choosing a role to play most hoaxers and poseurs fit on a personality which will bring them a mixture of approbation, authority and reflected glamour. Just as children 'play at doctors', impersonating a doctor still has a strong appeal for some adults. It's not a role which calls for any training— according to the image projected by television drama, you don't actually have to *do* anything at all.

You are either offhand and witty (James Robertson Justice in *Doctor in the House*), sage and sympathetic (Andrew Cruickshank in *Dr Finlay's Casebook*), goodlooking and soulful (Richard Chamberlain in *Dr Kildare*), or gruff and down to earth (*Owen, MD*). Most of us know the lines by heart: 'Where do you get the pain . . . just slip off your top things . . . now relax . . . does that hurt . . . take this along to the chemist's and if it doesn't get any better come back in a fortnight's time . . . no, the *other* door. Next. . . .'

A Guyanese mental hospital patient picked up so much of the patter in a Surrey hospital that he found it quite easy to work as a psychiatric doctor at four other hospitals. The judge, sending him to jail for five years, expressed himself horrified that the man should have been able to get away with his deception for so long. He obviously hadn't been reading the papers.

Another immigrant, a native of Afghanistan who had failed his medical exams, armed himself with a forged medical diploma from the University of Kabul and was employed at different times in twelve English hospitals. Altogether he conducted 150 operations for tonsils and adenoids. According to the General Medical Council it was the first time in ten years' screening of 25,000 overseas doctors that they had been deceived.

One wonders just how many medical poseurs are still working in British hospitals because the incidence of these impersonations is not perhaps as rare as the authorities seem to believe. In January 1974 another imposter was jailed for two years after working over a three-year period at the Royal Seabathing

Hospital, Ramsgate, the Luton and Dunstable Hospital and the Queen Elizabeth II Hospital at Welwyn Garden City. Although he was not a doctor and held no qualifications as a surgeon he treated hundreds of patients and a medical report said that he was addicted to the medical profession as a smoker is addicted to cigarettes.

Some impostures are so brilliant that they earn all the admiration that the perpetrator desperately seeks. Take the archetypal success story of Ferdinand Waldo Demara who by the time he was thirty had lived nine successful lives to the full. Born in 1922 he had played the roles of Trappist monk, naval surgeon, Christian Brother, deputy sheriff, psychologist, doctor, soldier and sailor.

Presenting false papers he got himself taken on as a surgeon lieutenant in the Canadian Navy and his first job was to extract a tooth for the ship's captain. Daunting? Not for Surgeon Lieutenant Cyr, as he then was: 'That night I read up on dentistry, next morning I shot the skipper's jaw full of novocain and out came the tooth. No trouble at all.' He thought nothing of performing lung resections or, during the Korean campaign, removing a bullet from within a fraction of an inch of a man's heart. While posing as a Professor of Biology he kept one jump ahead of the class by reading the textbook up the night before; as he said, 'the best way to learn anything is to teach it.'

What often surprises the layman is the ease with which a completely unqualified person can insinuate himself into a situation calling for great technological expertise. In the USA an ex-prisoner invented a whole string of qualifications for himself— BSc, MSc (aero-engineering), AMI (Mech)E, AMI(Chem)E, AMI(Elec)E and a doctorate in Nuclear Physics. Armed with these impressive qualifications and what he had been able to pick up from an elementary course in engineering taken while in jail for attempted bigamy, he was soon helping to design the C5-A, the world's largest military transport plane. 'Dr' Maitland's responsibility was for the structural integrity of the inner and outer wing pylons which were to support the engines, the fuel systems and the hydraulic system for wing mechanisms—for this work undertaken in 1967 he earned over £100 a week.

Subsequently he worked for various top level firms in America and Britain including Lockheeds, Handley Page and Westland's the helicopter firm. The *People*, reporting this remarkable story in February 1969, asked, 'How can a man fool his way into one of the top technological industries?' There appeared to be no facesaving answer.

Armed with the accepted diplomas, the accepted background, accent and poise, anyone it seems can get to the top without much bother. Like the Dublin convict who did a clerical refresher course at Trinity College. He found no difficulty in becoming resident Chaplain at the Dublin YWCA. Later he took over a Norfolk parish while the vicar was in hospital. Had he stuck to mere impersonation he might by now have become a Rt Rev. Suffragan Bishop, but overcome by temptation he began uttering stolen cheques and in October 1968 was removed from his cure.

The feudally minded British are inordinately impressed with anyone who appears to spring from the upper ranks of society. Even in these egalitarian times a man who claims to be an Eton and Oxford educated nobleman commands immediate deference. If he can hint at an ancient title, a medieval country seat and connections with royalty all defences are down.

For thirty-two years a man whom Fleet Street dubbed 'the King of the Con Men' traded on the well-founded assumption that however strange your behaviour, a resounding title will explain all. At various times in his career he posed as Lord Colchester, Lord Michael Ross-Sarel and Lord Harleeg. As befitting a Peer of the Realm he sported a monocle, was always surrounded by pretty women and drank champagne in the very best hotels. Sometimes he ran bogus film companies, at other times he acted as a film agent. Like many hereditary peers he was politically naïve—so naïve that he once started a multi-racial strip-club in Johannesburg and was deported to Swaziland for his impertinence.

In October 1969 he arrived at Oxford Quarter Sessions where his counsel was reduced to imploring the judge's pity: 'The lot of the middle-aged confidence trickster', he pleaded, 'is not an enviable one.' Towards the end 'Lord Colchester' had been reduced to taking paying guests into his '700-year-old farmhouse in the Cotswolds', an establishment as bogus as himself.

One of the most inventive of contemporary con men is Lt Col. Allen (alias Lord Antrim, Lord Harrington, Lord Hamilton, Lord Moyne, Capt. Hurst, Lord Vesnay, Commander Coxon, Lord Granard of Ardmore and Professor N. I. Hoskins) who in June 1967 rang up a West End jeweller and announced himself to be one of the Queen's equerries. Her Majesty wanted to present someone with a platinum and diamond brooch. Could the jeweller hasten to the Palace to discuss designs? He suggested a rendezvous in the Royal Mews to avoid the crowds watching the Changing of the Guard. The jeweller arrived at the Mews only too delighted to execute so regal a commission. He asked a policeman for the Colonel and an aristocratic figure in tweeds stepped forward and introduced himself. The jeweller gave him a £600 necklace on approval. Which is the end of the story.

But the ultimate end of all these stories is usually in the dock. On a bleak February day in 1973 the man the papers called Champagne Percy, yet another King of the Con Men, was told by Judge Oswell MacLeay that he was a menace to society. Seven years they gave him and by the time he comes out the world of bogus Lords and Ladies of caviare and champagne will be sadly changed.

The Americans are as gullible as the rest of us. A few years ago a most improbable couple, a twenty-five-year-old unemployed Canadian lumberjack and a fourteen-year-old runaway boy, imposed their way all over the States on an incredible safari of theft. Posing as the son of the then Canadian Prime Minister Lester Pearson, the lumberjack was given warm civic greetings by such dignitaries as Governor Lester Maddox of Georgia. He and the boy (always introduced as his valet) were provided with an escort for their Cadillac by US Government security men while they moved from gracious home to gracious home robbing as they went. When the police eventually caught up with them the Atlanta prosecutor said: 'It's extraordinary. As far as we can find out no one ever challenged this young man.'

There is even less temptation to question a person who offers you the chance of acquiring large sums of money for a relatively small outlay. The ease with which normally rational men and women can be deceived into thinking they are about to receive an inheritance has proved an almost foolproof source of money in the past and will undoubtedly continue to do so in the future. Using a telephone directory you select a fairly common name— Cooper for instance—and get in touch with as many Coopers as you can. Sir Travers Cooper, you tell them, a wealthy Australian sheepfarmer, died intestate in 1923 but left an estate now valued at over £1½ million pounds. A fighting fund is to be established to secure the money and distribute it to the rightful heirs among whom they are fortunately numbered.

You don't have to invent a mythical Sir Travers—you can use any old figure from history. Not so long ago a Mrs Whiteaker sold shares in the estate of Sir Francis Drake to several hundred guileless Iowans. The con was repeated but on a more grandiose scale by another American, Oscar Merril Hartzell. He invented an illegitimate son for Sir Francis Drake, whose heir had acquired a heritage of $22,000 million. Only Hartzell knew where the heir was and selected American businessmen were invited to subscribe to a fighting fund to regain the fortune. For every dollar invested five hundred would be repaid when the legal battle was won. Only people with the surname Drake or family connections with a Drake could contribute. He appointed agents through the Middle West and the money began to roll in at a rate of about $2,500 a week. All those who invested were sworn to secrecy—if the pledge was broken they forfeited their contribution and their expectations.

Now and again Hartzell released details of progress to his agents. At one stage he announced that the estate was worth £400,000 million, twenty times more than his original estimate. In the end some 70,000 victims had been enmeshed in the scheme. In 1933 Hartzell was extradited from the country to which he had fled and after a year and a half of preparing their case the FBI managed to secure a conviction. But even after he had been locked up people continued to subscribe, so unshakeable was their belief in the validity of the Drake claim. In the first eighteen months that Hartzell was in jail $350,000 dollars were sent in contributions to his chief agent.

136

A similar tempting offer was made by Estate Claims of America Inc. which in the 1960s was operating from an office in Providence, Rhode Island. Letters were sent to people in America and Britain with the surname of Sullivan, O'Brien and Gray announcing that three people, Frances Sullivan, Mary E. O'Brien and Edmund Gray had recently died intestate in the Providence area leaving just over £12,000. For a fee of twelve dollars they offered to provide Sullivans, O'Briens and Grays with documents which could help establish whether they were entitled to any part of the estate. The money came rolling in.

The largest sum involved in recent legacy frauds ran into millions. In 1965 Gerald Mallett, a forty-four-year-old Gravesend scaffolder was one of 22,000 Malletts who were persuaded that they might get a share of a £120 million fortune. The Malletts read that a Princess Ayoubi had organised a rally of people named Mallett or Malet at Limoges. Mr Mallett went to the rally and with others he heard the Princess, who claimed to be the widow of the Emir of Shahidan, an Iraqi oil magnate, describe how Jean-Pierre Malet, a poor peasant, had amassed a fortune in America, leaving £20 million when he died in 1818. Since then the money had been lying in a New York bank quietly accruing until now it was worth £120 million. The Princess, who said she was a great grand-daughter of one of Jean-Pierre's brothers, proposed to fight for the money on behalf of all the Malet descendants.

The Malletts, by painstaking research, proved that they were descended from Guilla de Mallett, a French soldier taken prisoner by the British during the Napoleonic wars. When the Princess was told this she assured them that they would get a substantial share of the New York millions. Most of their savings went on research and travelling and they appear to have given the Princess less than £3. An ex-schoolteacher, she was eventually indicted for fraud and forgery.

It is often difficult to untangle the motivating forces behind a deception. There are straightforward cases where the object is purely to make money; others grow from a desire to impart a spurious interest to the place where one lives. Ordnance Survey maps of the Hebrides are sprinkled with references to Prince

137

Charlie's Caves and had the far from bonny Pretender holed up in every one on his flight from Culloden he would never have got back to France at all.

The beds in which Queen Elizabeth slept, the oaks in which King Charles hid are part of an international pattern of historical invention which can be traced right back to Calvary—were all the pieces of the True Cross assembled they would probably reconstruct into something the size of the Eiffel Tower.

Lord Curzon during a tour of the Holy Land in the 1880s noted that bodies could be buried in several places without exciting undue surprise. There was Lazarus 'whose tomb I encountered first at Bethany and afterwards at Larnaka in Cyprus. Again we know that John the Baptist was beheaded; which may explain how it came about that I saw the mausoleum of his body in Samaria and of his head at Damascus. But it did not explain how, on another occasion, I came across the greater part of his remains at Genoa in Italy. The Virgin Mary has two graves, one in the Garden of Gethsemane and another at Ephesus.' But for Curzon the most curious find was two sepulchres of the mythical Noah: 'I had, I thought left him safely buried at Hebron, when later on, in the neighbourhood of Baalbek I came across him again interred in a tomb 40 yards long by two or three feet wide.'

Noah may be twice buried but the credulous still have hopes of finding his Ark. You may recall that in the Beginning God created Adam who lived for 930 years and begat Seth; Seth lived to be 912 and had Enos; Enos lived to be 905 and had Kenan; Kenan died at the age of 910 having begat Ma-hal alel; Ma-hal alel survived until he was 895 and begat Jared; Jared beat them all and having begat Enoch lasted for 962 years; Enoch fathered Methusaleh and was taken in the prime of life, a mere 365; Methusaleh begat Lamech and he begat Noah and Noah at the advanced age of 500 became the father of Shem, Ham and Japheth. It was Noah who was instructed by the Lord that in order to escape the impending flood he must make himself an ark of gopher wood 300 cubits long and take into it his family and two of every living thing.

It's a delightful fiction which finds echoes in Babylonian legend

138

where the travails of Utnapishtim bear striking resemblances to those of Noah. The Greeks have a similar story in which Deucalion escapes from a flood caused by Zeus and lands not on Mount Ararat but on Parnassus. Although you don't have to be an anthropologist to realise that none of these stories is factually accurate there are Christians who believe implicitly that somewhere on Mount Ararat the Ark still lurks, although why it has never been discovered is not explained.

The faith of such fundamentalists must have been strengthened heartily in February 1974 when Frank E. Moss, Chairman of the Senate Space Committee, told the American Congress on Surveying and Mapping that a spot on a photograph received from a US space satellite supported evidence that an object about 14,000 feet up Mount Ararat is Noah's Ark. 'It's about the right size and shape,' he said. There has not been much of a rush to go and look.

Wanting to be in the forefront of adventure has frequently led to deception; over-enthusiasm may cause an individual to engineer a fraud either for purposes of personal gain or to achieve lasting glory and fame.

Recently doubts have been cast on the memory of a great twentieth-century explorer. In the *Encyclopaedia Britannica* Richard Evelyn Byrd rates a full column, as well he might. Naval officer, explorer and scientist he became a folk hero to his fellow countrymen. He took off from King's Bay, Spitzbergen, at 12.50 a.m. on the morning of 9 May 1926, and with his co-pilot flew to the North Pole, a feat comparable in those days to landing on the moon. His three-engined Fokker plane named Josephine Ford became as famous as Apollo IX and Byrd and his fellow pilot Bennett were fêted, banqueted and festooned with decorations before they set off on a triumphal coast-to-coast tour.

Byrd had several reasons for wanting to reach the Pole on 9 May. When he arrived at King's Bay he found the fifty-four-year-old Norwegian explorer Roald Amundsen, who had already beaten Scott in the race to the South Pole, making plans to fly to the Pole in an airship. Byrd had invested $20,000 in his trip. He had newspaper contracts, he had been sponsored by the National Geographic Society and all eyes from President Calvin Coolidge down were upon him. So a wave of pride swept the States when Byrd announced he was the first man to fly over the North Pole.

But it now seems Byrd may not have been first; that distinction rests perhaps with Amundsen who made the trip a few days later and rates but half a page in *Britannica*. It has been worked out that Byrd couldn't possibly have flown from King's Bay to the Pole in 15½ hours—at 70 mph he could only have got to within a hundred or so miles of his objective. Doubts were first raised by Bernt Balchen, a Norwegian flyer whom Byrd hired to help fly the Josephine Ford through the States on its lap of honour. Balchen firmly believes that Byrd never completed the 1,500-mile trip. Soon after take-off the plane developed an oil leak and according to Balchen circled round and round out of sight and sound of King's Bay until a sufficiently reasonable time had elapsed to support a story of having flown to the Pole.

Balchen alleges that in 1928, just before he died, Byrd's co-pilot Bennett revealed the details of the hoax: 'We were just north of Spitzbergen', Bennett said, 'when the Commander discovered that oil leak. He became quite concerned about it and ordered me to fly back to the north coast of Spitzbergen—15 or 20 miles away. We discussed the possibility of flying over to East Greenland but he finally ordered me to fly back and forth and this is what we did until he told me to return to King's Bay.'

The story is supported by a detailed analysis made at Uppsala University in Sweden in 1960. A meteorologist, Professor Liljequist, worked out the Fokker's capabilities. Byrd had claimed that a fortuitous wind arose which had brought them back to King's Bay in record time. Professor Liljequist studied the Arctic weather charts for 9 May and found no evidence of a wind strong enough to support Byrd's story. Had Byrd really flown to the Pole, he claimed, the trip would have taken two hours longer. Byrd died in 1957 after directing five expeditions to the Antarctic, on one of which he became the first American to fly to the South Pole, an act which brought him further fame and the title of Rear Admiral, retired.

When the honours are so high the jockeying to establish a right to a First can be intense. If Byrd didn't actually fly to the Pole there is a precedent for the deception. In 1909 Frederick

140

Augustus Cook startled the world by announcing that he had
walked to the North Pole assisted by two Eskimos. He wrote a
book, *My Attainment To The Pole*, to prove it. Just as Byrd had
snatched the honours from Amundsen so Cook snatched them
from Robert Peary who returned from a successful journey to the
Pole a few days after Cook made his announcement. But Cook
was discredited by his companions; his claim was rejected by
Copenhagen University and Peary lived to gain his rightful
recognition. This wasn't the first attempt that Cook had made to
win admiration. Three years earlier he had led an expedition to
Mount McKinley in Alaska and claimed to have got to the top
although other explorers openly doubted his word. In 1922 Cook
was sentenced to fourteen years' imprisonment for fraud and in
1940 he died in the obscurity which he had taken such elaborate
pains to avoid.

Cook stood to gain a great deal of money from being the first
man to reach the North Pole on foot but there are other
impostures in which money is not the driving force. Soviet
Russia has frequently doctored the truth for ideological purposes
—people and events are removed permanently from the pages of
history without anyone seeming to find the deception comic.
Many educated people have an obsessive desire to be
remembered as innovators and quite frequently their forgeries
are accepted for considerable periods of time. It wasn't until 1953
that new techniques of analysis proved conclusively that the skull
discovered by an amateur geologist called Charles Dawson in
1912 was a fake—Eoanthropus Dawsoni which for over forty
years had been accepted as a human dating from Pleistocene
times was found to have the jawbone of an orang-outang.
Whoever assembled Piltdown Man, whether it was Dawson or an
accomplice, was motivated by a desire to set people talking. And
that may well be what lies behind the comparatively recent
production of a map calculated to prove that Norsemen sailed all
the way round Greenland.

In the autumn of 1965 I was one of a number of journalists
who attended a conference at which George Painter, Assistant
Keeper in charge of fifteenth-century printed books at the
British Museum, talked about a remarkable map of Vinland

which he and a team of experts had spent several years authenticating. The eleven by sixteen inch map was drawn on paper made in the Upper Rhineland about 1440 and its significance to scholars was that it showed not only the known medieval world but also Iceland, Greenland, and an island to the west of Iceland called Vinland Insula.

The map first came on the scene in 1957 when an Italian book dealer living in Spain sold it for $100,000 to a purchaser who eight years later donated it to the Yale library. At the time the Yale experts hailed it as 'the most exciting cartographic discovery of the century' because it established beyond doubt that the North-East American coast—or Vinland—had been visited by Lief Eriksson, the Viking explorer, long before the arrival of Christopher Columbus in 1492.

For nine years the Vinland Map was accepted and then Yale announced in February 1974 that far from being a fifteenth-century work, the map could not have been produced before the 1920s. Chemical analysis of 54 specks of ink showed that 'the likelihood of a pigment of the crystalline size and shape of that found in the Vinland Map ink being used in a map of A.D. 1440 can be compared with the likelihood that Admiral Nelson's flagship at Trafalgar was a hovercraft'.

It was the greatest embarrassment to scholars since Piltdown Man was downgraded to the status of an ape, but not everyone was convinced. George Painter of the British Museum was quoted as saying that he 'would stand by everything'. He said it was 'just another episode in the dialogue between scholars and investigators'.

Not unconnected with the Vinland Map forgery, if forgery it eventually proves to be, is a much cruder exhibit known as the Kensington Stone. It first came to light in 1898 west of the Great Lakes in the middle of America. The stone was inscribed with 221 characters which purported to be a message describing how in the year 1362 thirty Vikings on a voyage of discovery west from Vinland penetrated one thousand miles into the interior and were there attacked presumably by Red Indians.

The stone was genuine, the inscription false, probably carved by a couple of local farmers. But since it seemed to prove that the

142

Scandinavians reached the midwest a century before Columbus set out from Spain, it was welcomed enthusiastically by the largely Swedish inhabitants of Kensington, Minnesota. In 1921 a twenty-two-ton granite replica of the bogus runestone was set up in what more and more people were now convinced was the birthplace of modern America.

So successful was the fraud that in 1948 the most respected museum in the States, the Smithsonian Institution, gave it a twelve-month exhibition. In 1965, still revered, it was carted off to the New York World's Fair as one of Minnesota's prize relics. The stone, bought in 1911 for ten dollars, was probed by the Minnesota Historical Society and a report prepared by a five-member committee endorsed it as genuine.

Brian Branston of the BBC who investigated this still widely accepted forgery in 1973, told me that the residents of Kensington are unshaken in their belief that it dates from Viking times. Neither are they bothered by the derision of scholars, one of whom dismissed it with the comment 'it's like finding a telephone directory underneath a Viking ruin'. The stone forms part of a shrine in the local Chamber of Commerce and, not unnaturally, is a potent tourist attraction. It plays a similar role in Minnesota to the part played by the Loch Ness monster in the Highlands of Scotland.

Despite a complete absence of any but the flimsiest evidence that there is anything larger than a fish in the loch, belief in Nessie is imperishable; indeed since 1933, when a new road was built along the northern shore of the loch, sightings have increased dramatically. Nessie has been photographed on many occasions, even filmed. An amateur with a cine camera took some footage in 1960 and this was handed to the RAF for analysis. They seemed to think that there might be something there.

Every summer until their money ran out in 1972 volunteer members of the Loch Ness Phenomena Investigation Bureau were on watch with their powerful binoculars, cameras at the ready. They have had at least one 'conclusive' sighting. I have seen the film and the blurred indistinct shape in the water could have been anything—an upturned boat, a wave, perhaps even the tip of a ninety-foot log. Recently Field Enterprises Educational

Corporation of Chicago offered a grant of $20,000 to the Bureau and with their help a submersible explored the loch but Nessie still refused to prove herself.

Nessie fever is not confined to the British. In 1973 a consortium of Japanese businessmen raised £250,000 to send an eleven-man expedition to Scotland. The search party, headed by Tokyo impresario Mr Yoshio Kou, spent several weeks snorkeling in the waters of the loch and returned to the East without reporting a ripple of evidence.

In its archives the BBC has a remarkable collection of eye-witness accounts from a wide variety of people, all of whom are adamant that they have seen something which cannot be explained away as an upturned dinghy or a motorboat or a lump of driftwood. A Benedictine monk from the Abbey at Fort Augustus saw in 1935 'three considerable humps appear in line in the water' which then moved obliquely in a north-westerly direction.

Other people have seen humps, some have seen a head and a neck, one lucky woman saw the beast's great tail. Sometimes the monster undulates, at other times it ploughs through the loch faster than any motor launch and it can dive like a submarine always leaving the 'water like glass'. In 1964 I had a unique opportunity of talking to two men who with a third had been vouchsafed one of the most conclusive sightings ever recorded. They were both highly articulate, not the sort of men who are given to romanticising. Neither of them had ever seen anything strange in the loch before although they had lived alongside it all their lives. At about twenty to twelve one summer morning the three men, who had been rock-drilling above the loch, stopped work, collected their tools and were about to descend to the road below. Then, in the words of Sandy Russell:

'First of all I saw through the trees this object which appeared at first to be a boat. We watched it for about a minute before we realised it wasn't a boat, it was in fact moving too fast. It suddenly accelerated at tremendous speed and turned in towards the shore leaving a terrific wake.'

I asked Russell what colour it was:

'It was grey. After it turned into the shore it became

144

motionless and we watched it for a minute before it sank out of sight.'

'Supposing', I said to Russell, 'that somebody suggested to you that you had been watching some kind of optical illusion?'

'Oh no! Absolutely not! It couldn't possibly be. I mean we watched the thing for fully three minutes from the time we first noticed it until it sank out of sight under the waves. And after it sank out of sight the loch was completely calm like a mirror again.'

After I'd talked with Sandy Russell at Fort Augustus I drove down the road to Invermoriston and talked to John Mackenzie, the second of the two men involved in the events of the previous Thursday morning. I came away completely convinced that both men believed they had seen exactly what they described. I was equally convinced that what they had seen was some kind of optical illusion.

The important thing about monsters is that they must by definition be hugely awe-inspiring. Nobody is going to get worked up about some strange prehistoric survival six inches long. Even the Yeti, the abominable snowman who is reputed to haunt the Himalayas, is a sizeable beast with terrifyingly large footprints. Nessie yields a blurred shape on a negative, the Yeti yields footprints and a few hairs. Both creatures have their origins in myth—reports of a monster in Loch Ness go back to the fifth century—but Nessie is the sole survivor of a vast army of water-horses which inhabited the Highlands and Islands of Scotland in the heyday of romance and legend. Significantly, a lorry driver who thought he had sighted the monster was interviewed by the BBC in 1938. Pressed to say what he had seen, he hesitated and then: 'It remembered me', he said, 'of an old horse.'

Whenever I gaze across the dark waters of Loch Ness I am remembered of a Scottish poet and schoolmaster called Robert Henryson who had a fine pen and a macabre sense of humour. In the deep snowy winter of 1506 he lay in his chamber dying of a flux. He was visited in his extremity by a noted local witch. Pointing out of the window at an oak tree in the orchard she said that if Henryson would but go and walk thrice round the tree repeating the words 'whikey tree, whikey tree, take away this flux from me' he would presently be cured.

The poet looked at her for a long time in silence, then he raised himself from his pillows and he spoke. Irreverent and defiant, his words ring down the centuries. 'Good dame, I might do better', he said, 'if I were to walk round that oak table thrice and cry "oken burd, oken burd garre me shit a hard turde".' And so saying he lay back and expired.

I think of Master Henryson when people tell me they've seen the Loch Ness monster; when they want me to help them open Joanna Southcott's Box or purchase for 15p the key to eternal life. The witch had the last laugh when they buried the old man; that, she no doubt said, is what happens to those who don't have faith in the old ways. But Henryson had something more valuable than faith: he had doubt and doubting he died. A splendid way to go.